327

A-LEVEL YEAR 2

STUDENT GUIDE

EDEXCEL

Politics

Global politics

John Jefferies

Series e

HODDER
EDUCATION
AN HACHETTE UK COMPANY

Hodder Education, an Hachette UK company, Blenheim Court, George Street, Banbury, Oxfordshire OX16 5BH

Orders

Bookpoint Ltd, 130 Park Drive, Milton Park, Abingdon, Oxfordshire OX14 4SB

tel: 01235 827720

fax: 01235 400401

email: education@bookpoint.co.uk

Lines are open 9.00 a.m.–5.00 p.m., Monday to Saturday, with a 24-hour message answering service. You can also order through the Hodder Education website: www.hoddereducation.co.uk

© John Jefferies 2018

ISBN 978-1-4718-9309-4

First printed 2018

Impression number 5 4 3

Year 2022 2021 2020 2019

This Guide has been written specifically to support students preparing for the Edexcel A-level Politics examinations. The content has been neither approved nor endorsed by Edexcel and remains the sole responsibility of the author.

With thanks to Eric Hadley for his help with this Student Guide.

Cover photograph: Kristaps Eberlins/123RF

Typeset by Integra Software Services Pvt. Ltd., Pondicherry, India

Printed in India

Hachette UK's policy is to use papers that are natural, renewable and recyclable products and made from wood grown in sustainable forests. The logging and manufacturing processes are expected to conform to the environmental regulations of the country of origin.

Contents

■Getting the most from this book

Exam tips

Advice on key points in the text to help you learn and recall content, avoid pitfalls, and polish your exam technique in order to boost your grade.

Knowledge check

Rapid-fire questions throughout the Content Guidance section to check your understanding.

Knowledge check answers

1 Turn to the back of the book for the Knowledge check answers.

Summaries

- Each core topic is rounded off by a bullet-list summary for quick-check reference of what you need to know.

Exam-style questions

Sample student answers

Practise the questions, then look at the student answers that follow.

Commentary on sample student answers

Read the comments (preceded by the icon **e**) showing how many marks each answer would be awarded in the exam and exactly where marks are gained or lost.

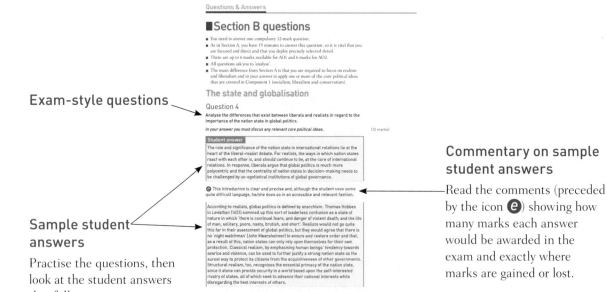

■ About this book

The aim of this Student Guide is to prepare you for Edexcel Politics A-level Paper 3, **Global Politics**. This paper comprises a third of the Politics A-level, and all of the topics covered in this guide could be examined in the exam. It is therefore vital that you are familiar and confident with all the material.

The **Content Guidance** section covers all six topics in the Edexcel A-level specification, Global Politics component:

- Theories of global politics
- The state and globalisation
- Global governance: political and economic
- Global governance: human rights and environmental
- Power and developments
- Regionalism and the European Union

You should use the Content Guidance to ensure you are familiar with all the key concepts and terms, statistics, issues and arguments. It is also important that you learn a range of relevant examples so that you can quote them in your answers. This will demonstrate that you possess a really detailed understanding of the material and will provide your answers with real conviction. Throughout this section there is a series of Knowledge checks, which you should use to ensure that you fully understand a topic before moving on to the next one. The answers to these Knowledge checks can be found at the end of the guide. The advice in the Exam tips boxes is designed to help you avoid significant common errors made by students, as well as guiding you towards good practice.

The **Questions & Answers** section is an opportunity to develop your exam technique so that you become conversant with the sorts of exam skills the examiners will reward.

This guide does not provide a full range of examples or go into full detail, so you should use it alongside other resources, such as your class notes, the *Global Politics for A-level* textbook by Robert Murphy, John Jefferies and Josie Gadsby, as well as articles in *Politics Review* (both published by Hodder Education). You should also use a variety of websites — such as those of the BBC, Al Jazeera, the *Guardian*, *Huffington Post* and *Washington Post* — in order to keep up to date with current news. Global politics is a constantly evolving subject and the more knowledgeable you are about contemporary developments in international relations, the more you will enjoy the subject and the more confident your writing will become.

Content Guidance

■ Theories of global politics

Main ideas of realism

Realism is a political philosophy that attempts to explain how global politics can best be understood. According to classical realism, human beings — and consequently nation states — are motivated by a desire for power and security. Niccolò Machiavelli (1469–1527) in *The Prince* (1513) declared that humans are 'insatiable, arrogant, crafty and shifting, and above all malignant, iniquitous, violent and savage'. The realist thinker Hans Morgenthau accepted this, pessimistically stating that 'the social world is but a projection of human nature on to the collective plane'.

Structural or neo-realists further argue that since nation states are the principal actors in international relations and since their primary motivation is one of self-interest, global politics is necessarily anarchic. As a result of this states compete for influence, thus creating inherent instability within the system. Morality and ideology therefore play no part in power politics. As the Victorian prime minister Lord Palmerston put it, 'We have no eternal allies, and we have no perpetual enemies. Our interests are eternal and perpetual, and those interests it is our duty to follow.'

States as key actors in global politics and the balance of power (state sovereignty)

The realist approach to global politics is highly practical. As the key actors in global politics, nation states do not act out of an altruistic desire to make the world a better place. Instead, they seek to establish a balance of power that works in their favour and ensures their security.

- Defensive realists, such as Kenneth Waltz, emphasise that nation states are most influenced by the need for security. Nation states therefore are 'security maximisers'.
- Offensive realists, such as John Mearsheimer, argue that nation states are more predatory and, as power-maximisers, seek influence as well as security.

Since nation states are the dominant force in global politics, they cannot appeal to any higher authority to protect their interests. As John Mearsheimer puts it, there is no 'night watchman'. This means that in a potentially hostile world order, nation states need to achieve a balance of power that protects their interests and independence. A balance of power can thus establish a stable equilibrium that reduces the potential for conflict.

International anarchy and its implications

Since there is no superior authority to which nation states are equally accountable, international relations are **anarchic**. This does not mean that there is complete

Realism According to realism, nation states play the dominant role in international politics and make decisions based on maximisation of their power and security. States thus exist in a 'self-help environment' and so are guided by pragmatic considerations of self-interest.

Knowledge check 1

What are the main principles of the realist approach to global politics?

International anarchy means that there is no supranational authority that can impose rules on nation states. Since international relations are, therefore, conducted without enforceable laws, states can act according to their own interests, creating a state of international anarchy.

confusion, nor that what Thomas Hobbes referred to in *Leviathan* (1651) as a state of nature exists. What it does mean is that there is no supranational authority that can enforce a global rule of law. Nation states are therefore responsible for their own interests, so they exist in a self-help environment in which their security depends upon their military power and the alliances they make. Statecraft is thus the way in which nation states achieve the best possible outcome for themselves in a hostile environment in which there are no rules.

Inevitability of war

According to realism, conflict is inherent in international relations. The reasons for this include:

- Nation states seek power, influence and security. According to Hans Morgenthau, 'the struggle for power is universal in time and space'.
- Since nation states continually seek to advance their own interests, instability and uncertainty are inherent within the global system since no state can know for certain the intentions of another state.
- States co-operate only when it is in their national interest to do so.
- There is no authority greater than the nation state that can compel obedience to a global rule of law.

The security dilemma

The way in which nation states seek to protect and advance their interests creates a **security dilemma**. This is because, by trying to achieve a balance of power in its favour, a nation state will make other nation states feel vulnerable, so that they *also* have to increase their power in order to protect their security. The concept of the security dilemma thus challenges the extent to which a balance of power can maintain peace, since by trying to increase their security nation states may actually make themselves more vulnerable by encouraging a volatile and unstable struggle for power.

Main ideas of liberalism

Liberalism rejects what it sees as the unnecessary pessimism of realism. According to liberalism, human beings and nation states are not simply motivated by the desire for power and security. Instead, nation states can work together in harmony in order to achieve a collective good. Liberals agree that the international system is anarchic. They argue, however, that nation states appreciate that by co-operating with each other they can all achieve relative gains, so that international relations are not zero-sum. Conflict is therefore not inherent within the system.

According to liberalism, states are also not the only key players in global politics. Instead they share power with intergovernmental organisations (IGOs) and non-governmental organisations (NGOs) so that international relations are more than simply the way in which nation states react with each other. Furthermore, the way in which the interests of nation states and **non-state actors** can often be the same creates a world of complex interdependence in which co-operation, rather than conflict, provides the default position for global relations.

Knowledge check 2

Why do realists believe that conflict is inherent within global politics?

Security dilemma
By building up their military and diplomatic influence in order to create a balance of power in their favour, nation states provoke other nation states to build up their own military forces to protect themselves. Consequently, this actually undermines their security by leading to an arms race.

Non-state actors
Organisations that play a significant role in international relations. They include IGOs, transnational corporations (TNCs), NGOs, global terrorist and crime networks, and religious movements.

The significance of morality and optimism in human nature

Liberalism is based upon an optimistic view of human nature. Whereas realists work from the premise that human beings are selfish and self-serving, liberals emphasise our capacity for co-operation and mutual interdependence. Since human beings can work together in shared enterprises and construct societies based upon the protection of their members, so nation states can co-operate in order to achieve the common good. Moral considerations, therefore, can also motivate the behaviour of states, rather than solely pragmatic considerations of self-gain.

Possibility of harmony and balance

According to the philosopher Immanuel Kant (1724–1804), it is possible to achieve a harmony of interests within a nation state through representative institutions and the rule of law. 'Perpetual peace' between states can also be achieved, if:

- all states protect the rights of their citizens
- states work together to achieve a collective good
- the rights of citizens everywhere are universally respected

Liberals thus argue that it is possible to achieve harmony and balance both within nation states and in global relations if nation states obey Kant's principles. This has more recently been called the democratic peace theory, whereby nation states — which base themselves on the rule of law rather than on an egotistical desire for self-gain — make the rational decision that they will benefit more through co-operation than through conflict.

Knowledge check 3

What are the main principles of the liberal approach to global politics?

Complex interdependence

Robert Keohane and Joseph Nye have argued that global relations have been transformed by the ever-closer connectivity between nation states and societies. This is due to the complex interdependence that is being established between states through economic globalisation and through shared responses to collective dilemmas such as climate change, terrorism and rogue states. Multiple channels of communication between states through transnational organisations, IGOs and NGOs thus establish the conditions for a more collective response to international relations. According to this theory, the realist approach to global politics — which emphasises the power-maximisation and security interests of one state — is rendered obsolete by the shared interests of states becoming so connected and overlapping.

Complex interdependence
A liberal concept that suggests the fortunes of nation states are inextricably connected through multiple channels, encouraging co-operation rather than conflict.

Impact and growth of international organisations

Since the end of the Second World War, the impact of international organisations in determining global policy has dramatically increased. Significant non-state actors include IGOs, NGOs and transnational corporations, all of which play an increasingly important role in international relations.

Intergovernmental organisations are institutions within which nation states can co-operate in order to achieve mutually beneficial outcomes. Such organisations include:

- United Nations: the United Nations is the world's most advanced organ of intergovernmental co-operation. It carries out a wide variety of judicial, security and development roles.

Knowledge check 4

What is the significance of collective dilemmas in global politics?

- World Bank, International Monetary Fund and World Trade Organization (Bretton Woods Institutions): the Bretton Woods Institutions encourage a neo-classical free-trade/free-market approach to economic development.
- Organisation for Economic Co-operation and Development: the 35 member states of the OECD are generally high-income countries, all of which are committed to democracy and free-market economics.
- G7 (G8 until Russia was suspended because of its annexation of Crimea in 2014) and G20: the Group of Seven and Group of Twenty regularly meet to discuss a collective response to global challenges. The G7 comprises the biggest economies in the Global North and the G20 the biggest economies in both the developing and developed world.
- Regional organisations: these include the European Union (EU), in which supranational elements of governance have been most highly developed, as well as others in which sovereignty has been less deeply pooled, such as the Association of Southeast Asian Nations (ASEAN).
- Interpol: the 190 nation states that are members of the International Police Organization share intelligence and resources in order to better combat international crime, drug trafficking and terrorism.

Non-governmental organisations (NGOs) are not-for-profit organisations that seek to influence the actions of nation states through soft power persuasion. They are widely consulted by governments and IGOs and so have become 'stakeholders' in global dialogue. They include:

- Greenpeace: a global pressure group that lobbies governments and IGOs to protect the environment
- Médecins Sans Frontières: a humanitarian group that provides medical help in conflict zones around the world

Transnational corporations are powerful businesses that have economic interests in many different countries and whose management possesses a regional or global outlook. In a globalised world, the economic decisions that TNCs make will have huge consequences for nation states and so they are increasingly involved in international decision-making. For instance:

- Google's negotiations with the People's Republic of China (2017) over whether it can be assured sufficient freedom to reopen operations in China
- Apple's discussions with the government of Narendra Modi (2017) about the terms of a trade deal in which it might start constructing iPhones in India

Likelihood of global governance

All of these non-state actors demonstrate the way in which states can work with and through other organisations. However, the effectiveness of **global governance** is undermined by the way in which, in most cases, nation states retain the dominant role in decision-making:

- On the United Nations Security Council, the Permanent Five possess the veto on security issues, illustrating the way in which nation states exercise a dominant role in decision-making.

Exam tip

This chapter introduces a lot of precise terms, such as 'security dilemma', 'balance of power' and 'complex interdependence'. Do utilise this sort of precise terminology in your work, because it will provide your writing with real conviction.

Global governance refers to the way in which decisions are increasingly made above the level of the nation state. This is through intergovernmental organisations and by the way in which nation states work with non-governmental and transnational organisations in order to resolve collective dilemmas.

- The United Nations' commitment to 'Responsibility to Protect' (2005) has proved a dead letter in conflicts such as the Syrian Civil War, since the Security Council and other key players, such as Turkey and Iran, have not been able to agree to a concerted approach.
- Both the International Court of Justice (World Court) and International Criminal Court rely upon the co-operation of nation states if their judgements are to be accepted and enforced.
- The proposals that are made at meetings of the G7 and G20 are only declarations of intent and have no enforcement power.
- Most regional organisations have comparatively little supranational authority over their members. Even the most advanced form of regionalism, the European Union, possesses a mechanism — Article 50 of the Lisbon Treaty — whereby a member state may leave the organisation.
- The decision by the Trump administration to pull the United States out of the UN Paris Climate Change Agreement further demonstrates the primary role that states play in international relations.

> **Knowledge check 5**
>
> Provide examples of attempts to develop global governance and explain why it is so difficult to achieve.

Divisions between realism and liberalism

Human nature and power

Realism and liberalism fundamentally differ in the way in which they view human nature and power.

According to realists, human beings are primarily motivated by self-centred desires. Nation states, consequently, are also seen as being driven by selfish desires and, in global relations, as always seeking to maximise their own power and security. As a result of this, international politics is anarchic since all states seek what is in their own best interests.

Liberals argue that realism is overly negative in its assessment of human nature and what motivates the actions of nation states. According to liberalism, co-operation is as inherent in human nature as conflict and so states also can be prepared to work together in order to achieve common ends.

Order and security and the likelihood of conflict

The liberal emphasis on complex interdependence and a shared response to collective dilemmas through IGOs thus suggests that states are not simply out to maximise their security and influence, as realists have argued. Instead, states can co-operate in order to resolve collective dilemmas. Liberals thus emphasise that global politics does not simply have to be seen as a game of 'winners and losers' and that nation states can collectively win if they are prepared to work together.

Realists respond that, since nation states exist within an anarchic structure of global politics, they cannot rely upon an 'international emergency call' to get them out of trouble. They therefore rely upon their power and influence in order to achieve their desired outcomes. Since all states prioritise the interests of their citizens, agreements and alliances between states will always be shifting and temporary.

Impact of international organisations and the significance of states

The possibility of greater global governance has been advanced by the rise of non-state actors. These have often played an important role in achieving a regional or global response to collective dilemmas:

- In 2009, the G20 agreed not to respond to the global economic crisis by imposing tariffs on foreign goods since this would negatively impact the global community.
- At the Paris Climate Change Conference in 2015, the United Nations achieved a global consensus on the importance of nation states working together to limit their carbon emissions in order to limit climate change.
- Regional organisations have, to a greater or lesser extent, pooled the sovereignty of their members. The European Union, for example, has a common citizenship and a single currency (Maastricht Treaty 1992) and a legal identity (Lisbon Treaty 2007), meaning it can negotiate on equal terms with nation states.
- All 47 members of the European Council have accepted the principles of the European Convention on Human Rights, which is adjudicated by the European Court of Human Rights in Strasbourg.

The centrality of states in international relations remains the bedrock of global politics, however. Therefore, although nation states may co-operate with other nation states through IGOs when it suits them, when their interests are threatened they will often resort to unilateral rather than collective action:

- In 2014, Russia annexed Crimea in defiance of international condemnation, including its suspension from the G8.
- In 2016, when a UN international tribunal declared that China's construction of artificial reefs in the Spratly Islands was against international maritime law, China refused to accept the jurisdiction of the court.
- In 2017, President Trump announced that the United States was withdrawing from the Paris Climate Change Agreement (2015) since the treaty is 'an agreement that disadvantages the United States to the exclusive benefit of other countries'.

Main ideas of the anarchical society and society of states theory

The realist and liberal approaches to international relations can seem to be unhelpfully diametrically opposed. Hedley Bull (1932–85), however, in The *Anarchical Society* (1977), attempted to reconcile these two viewpoints by suggesting a global framework based upon a '**society of states**'. This interpretation accepts that the liberal desire for global governance does not yet exist, but equally it challenges the realist assumption that states seek only their own immediate advantage. If that were so we would be a world of North Koreas, which is clearly not the case. Instead, states can build up trust with other states and establish powerful norms of reciprocal behaviour based upon mutually beneficial outcomes. This does not amount to global governance, since states remain the key decision-makers and can act unilaterally when they perceive it is in their best interests so to do. Nevertheless, the more that states adopt a collective approach to problem-resolution, the less anarchic international relations become.

Anarchical society and **society of states** Anarchical society and the society of states recognise the realist emphasis on the self-interest of nation states, while acknowledging that the interplay between states is governed by certain mutually advantageous rules and conventions that promote stability rather than anarchy.

To what extent do realism and liberalism explain post-2000 developments in global politics?

Whether global politics has become more interdependent in order to resolve collective dilemmas or has reverted to a more realist assessment of immediate national advantage is controversial. Table 1 illustrates how both interpretations can be justified by events since 2000.

Table 1 Liberal and realist approaches to global politics since 2000

Examples of liberalism	Examples of realism
UN Millennium (2000–15) and Sustainable (2015–30) Development Goals.	2014: Russian annexation of Crimea.
2002: establishment of the International Criminal Court.	2016: South Africa declared its intention to leave the International Criminal Court as membership is not in its national interest.
2005: United Nations World Summit endorsed 'Responsibility to Protect'.	2017: United States' withdrawal from the Paris Climate Change Agreement.
2007: Lisbon Treaty further developed the supranational elements of the European Union.	Chinese reef-building in South China Sea in defiance of international law.
2009: G20 agreed not to resort to protectionism as a response to the global economic crisis.	In response to the migrant and terrorist crises some members of the Schengen Agreement, which permits passport-free travel within the EU, have re-imposed border controls to protect their citizens.
2011: UN Resolution 1973 authorised military action to stop Libyan government attacks on its citizens.	Lack of a global consensus on how to resolve the Syrian Civil War (2011–): Russia, Turkey and Iran placing their geo-strategic interests first in the conflict.
2015: Climate Change Agreement signed in Paris as a result of a global consensus.	President Trump's pledge to build a wall between Mexico and the United States to stop illegal migration and drugs trafficking.

Exam tip

Throughout your course, keep a record of new developments in global politics and decide whether each represents a liberal or realist approach to international relations. This will ensure that your writing is always refreshingly up to date.

Summary

When you have completed this topic you should have a thorough knowledge of the following information and issues:
- The realist interpretation of international relations.
- The liberal interpretation of international relations.
- Why realists believe that global politics tends towards conflict.
- The meaning and significance of complex interdependence.
- Examples of the ways in which non-state actors have advanced global governance.
- The factors that obstruct the further development of global governance.
- Examples of co-operation and conflict in international relations.
- The significance of the 'society of states' thesis.
- Post-2000 examples of realism and liberalism in international relations.

In addition, you should have gathered appropriate information to help you answer the following wide-ranging questions:
1 Examine why realism and liberalism interpret international relations in such different ways.
2 Evaluate the extent to which global governance is successful.
3 Examine the ways in which global relations tend towards either a realist or a liberal model.
4 Evaluate the extent to which contemporary global politics is anarchic.

■ The state and globalisation

Characteristics of a nation state and of national sovereignty

Nation state — a political community bound together by citizenship and nationality

The concept of a **nation state** as a shared community bound together by nationality and citizenship has developed since the sixteenth century. William Shakespeare was acutely aware of a sense of collective history and shared cultural values that defined what it meant to be English. In *Henry V*, for example, Agincourt is portrayed as a national triumph against overwhelming odds, 'We few, we happy few, we band of brothers', and in *Richard II* John of Gaunt refers to England as 'This happy breed of men, this little world, This precious stone set in a silver sea'.

During the nineteenth century, a sense of shared national heritage helped to provoke the 1848 Revolutions and Otto von Bismarck (1815–98) cleverly exploited nationalism in order to achieve the unification of Germany (1871). The unification of Italy (1860) also depended upon a developing sense of national identity, while historians have suggested that the American Civil War (1861–65) forged a new sense of American identity.

At the Treaty of Versailles (1919), US president Woodrow Wilson further developed the concept of a nation state. According to the principle of 'self-determination', viable nation states shared a common ethnic heritage — a concept that led to the dismantling of the Austro-Hungarian Empire and its replacement with more ethnically homogenous nation states, such as Poland, Hungary and Austria.

Following the end of the Second World War, nationalist movements from Africa to the Far East challenged European empires, leading to decolonisation. In 1991 when the Soviet Union collapsed, its 15 constituent parts — such as Russia, Georgia, Ukraine and the Baltic States — became independent nation states based upon shared national characteristics.

The principle that nation states share collective values and ethnicity and a desire for nationhood continues to be highly significant in international relations:

- In 1993, Czechoslovakia broke up into the ethnically and culturally distinct Czech and Slovak Republics.
- The Palestine Liberation Organization (PLO) demands the right, as representatives of a distinct ethnic and political group, to statehood.
- Kurdish separatists in Turkey, Iraq, Syria, Iran and Armenia all claim the right to be part of a Kurdish state.

National sovereignty — the state's absolute power over citizens and subjects

A nation state possesses **sovereignty** over all those things that occur within its borders. This principle underpins the realist approach to international relations

> **Nation state** A sovereign body, the citizens of which share a recognisably homogenous culture, language and ancestry.

> **Sovereignty** The principle of unlimited authority. It is the key characteristic of a nation state and means that no other institution can arbitrarily impose its will on a sovereign state.

whereby nation states, whatever their size and strength, possess equal 'external sovereignty'. As a result of this, no state can legitimately interfere within the borders of another state.

The principle of equal sovereignty was first recognised by the Peace of Westphalia (1648), which ended the Thirty Years' War. This established the principle that Catholic and Protestant states could not use religion as a justification to intervene in other states, so developing the concept of inviolable borders. Article 2 of Chapter I of the United Nations Charter (1945) provides a modern interpretation of this concept, stating that 'The Organization is based on the principle of the sovereign equality of all its Members.'

The process of globalisation: a complex web of interconnectedness interlinking people, countries, institutions, culture, economics, technology and politics

Globalisation is the means by which a multi-layered web of complex interdependence is established that challenges the primacy of the nation state as the main organ of decision-making. There are many factors driving globalisation, including economics, finance, politics, technology and culture.

Economic globalisation

Since the end of the Cold War in 1991, economic globalisation has transformed the international economy. Often referred to as the Washington Consensus, economic globalisation encourages the spread of free-market neo-classical economic theory across the world. The Bretton Woods Institutions (the World Bank, International Monetary Fund and World Trade Organization) have all encouraged nation states to open up their markets to foreign trade, so 'flattening out' (Thomas Friedman) the global economy. As a result of this, the economies of nation states have become so closely connected through trade that a globalised economy has been created, which limits the choice of nation states if they are to attract foreign trade and investment. High tariffs and high corporate taxes would, for example, be likely to deter foreign capital and business, so the free market has become the default position for both developed and developing states.

Financial globalisation

The growing influence of global financial markets, encouraged by instantaneous internet communication, means that a nation state cannot insulate itself from the movement of global capital — unless it fully divorces itself from the international economy, as North Korea has done. In September 2008, the bankruptcy of the American investment bank Lehman Brothers led to stock markets across the globe plummeting, leading to a dramatic reduction in global trade. For example, Japanese exports declined by 57 per cent between August 2008 and January 2009, and in 2008–09 German exports declined by 25 per cent. The Chancellor of the Exchequer at the time, Alistair Darling, even admitted that the financial crisis brought the UK banking system to 'within hours' of collapse.

Knowledge check 6

What is the nation state and why is it important in global politics?

Globalisation The process by which the world becomes more closely linked, challenging the autonomy of nation states and creating greater connectivity between states and their citizens.

Economic globalisation The process by which the economies of nation states across the world become more closely connected through free trade. This principle is also referred to as the 'Washington Consensus'.

Political globalisation

As a result of **political globalisation**, the centrality of the state in decision-making has been challenged by the growing influence of non-state actors. These new 'stakeholders' in international dialogue, debate and decision-making complement and even challenge the traditionally dominant influence of nation states. For example, non-governmental organisations (NGOs), such as Greenpeace, now contribute to the global debate, and decisions that influence the nation state are often now taken through intergovernmental organisations (IGOs) such as the United Nations, World Bank, International Monetary Fund and World Trade Organization. Regional organisations, such as the European Union, have further dispersed power away from nation states through the pooling of sovereignty.

Internet (technology)

The internet advances financial, economic and political globalisation. This is because capital can now instantly pass from one state to another, making borders virtually meaningless. The global flow of digital information more than doubled from 2013 to 2015, to approximately 290 terabytes per second. In addition to this, the instantaneous exchange of information has created the potential for a genuinely global debate, making it much more difficult for a nation state to influence the information that its citizens receive.

The internet also provides the opportunity for global phenomena, such as the worldwide Pokémon GO craze in 2016 and the fidget spinner craze in 2017. More negatively, the internet enables crime syndicates to operate globally. Islamist-inspired terrorism can also be committed anywhere in the world: within days of each other, in May and June 2017, atrocities were committed in London, Manchester, Kabul and Tehran.

Cultural globalisation

As a result of the free flow of information, a more culturally homogenised global culture has been created. The advance of **cultural globalisation** has meant that those things that make cultures unique become less significant than those things that encourage uniformity. For example, 50 per cent of internet traffic is now in English and an Americanised world culture has increasingly focused on materialistic fulfilment and global brand-recognition. Brendan Barber has referred to this as a 'McWorld', indicating the way in which cultural differences are flattened out, so creating a much less diverse and more culturally uniform global society.

A growing number of companies possess global recognition, such as Coca-Cola, Apple, Walt Disney and Microsoft, demonstrating the way in which the consumer choices people make all over the world are influenced by the same brands. This has contributed to what has been called a **monoculture**, in which the **homogenisation** of once-diverse cultures and identities creates a striking uniformity of cultural experience wherever one travels in the world.

Knowledge check 7

In what ways is cultural globalisation controversial?

Political globalisation refers to the way in which nation states co-operate with other nation states and non-state actors in multilateral policy-making. Decisions are therefore made in a polycentric manner rather than simply by nation states acting alone.

Cultural globalisation The process by which what makes the culture of a nation state unique is challenged by the rise of a homogenised global culture, in which the cultural similarities between people across the world become more notable than the differences.

Homogenisation and **monoculture** These terms are similar to cultural globalisation and indicate a flattening out of the cultural differences between nation states. They are closely associated with materialism and consumerism and have been referred to as 'Coca-Colonization', suggesting a bland global cultural uniformity.

What has been the impact of globalisation on the state system?

Widening and deepening interconnectedness and interdependence

'No man is an island,

Entire of itself,

Every man is a piece of the continent,

A part of the main.'

John Donne (1572–1631)

'In the globalised world that is ours, maybe we are moving towards a global village, but that global village brings in a lot of different people, a lot of different ideas, lots of different backgrounds, lots of different aspirations.'

Marshall McLuhan (1911–80) in *War and Peace in the Global Village* (1968)

These two sentiments provide a good way of understanding the impact of globalisation on the state system. Nation states cannot escape being closely connected economically, politically and culturally with each other. The way in which nation states trade together, share instantaneous communications and co-operate through IGOs increasingly encourages global interdependence. The way, too, in which collective dilemmas such as climate change and terrorism cannot be resolved by nation states acting alone further encourages greater interdependence and interconnectedness. People all over the world can also instantaneously communicate with each other, as well as following the same celebrities, watching the same YouTube clips and buying the same brand products. Together, these all combine to challenge the borders and barriers that have hitherto made nation states the main actors in global politics.

The ways in which the development of international law challenges state control over citizens

In global politics, the state has traditionally determined the nature and extent of its citizens' civil liberties. **Westphalian principles** of non-interventionism have also enshrined the principle that there can be no legal justification to intervene in the internal affairs of a state.

According to liberals, however, the global community of nations should be guided by a universal standard of human rights. These have been encapsulated in core documents such as the United Nations Declaration of Human Rights (1948) and the European Declaration of Human Rights (1950), both of which possess considerable moral authority. A growing number of supranational judicial bodies have also been established to represent a global standard of international law:

- The International Court of Justice (or World Court) (1946) sits permanently at The Hague and was established to settle disputes between nation states and to provide advisory opinions on international disputes.

Westphalian principles refer to the concept developed by the Peace of Westphalia (1648) that states are sovereign in their domestic affairs. This means that attempts by other states to intervene within a sovereign state are illegal.

- The European Court of Human Rights (1959) sits in Strasbourg and rules on cases involving the European Convention on Human Rights.
- United Nations war crimes tribunals have been set up on an *ad hoc* basis. They have aimed to bring justice to victims of war crimes and human rights abuses committed in the former Yugoslavia, Cambodia, Rwanda and Sierra Leone.
- The International Criminal Court was established in 2002 as a permanent body to try individuals (including heads of state) accused of war crimes or crimes against humanity.

In addition to these tribunals and courts, NGOs such as Human Rights Watch have increased global awareness of human rights abuses. Advances in technology, such as photographing and filming on mobile phones, have further ensured that human rights abuses can be instantly publicised to a global audience.

Humanitarian and forcible intervention

Since the end of the Cold War, there has also been a rise in humanitarian/forcible interventions within sovereign states if their governments are abusing, or can no longer protect the human rights of, their citizens. These interventions include:

- safe havens in Iraq (1991)
- Kosovo (1999)
- Sierra Leone (1999)
- East Timor (2000)
- Libya (2011)
- Côte d'Ivoire (2011)

In 2005, at its World Summit, the United Nations published 'Responsibility to Protect', which recognised the principle that if a national government could no longer protect its citizens, the international community had the responsibility or duty to intervene on a moral imperative.

The differences between the realist and liberal approaches to globalisation

Liberals are optimistic about globalisation. Because of their focus on international co-operation, liberals see globalisation as a way of furthering the interconnectedness between peoples and nation states, so breaking down barriers and encouraging global responses to collective dilemmas. According to the Dell Theory of Conflict Resolution, by dramatically increasing global trade, economic globalisation reduces the chance of conflict. This is because, if all nation states are incorporated in the same international supply chain, war will inevitably lead to mutually assured economic destruction. This therefore means that it is not in the interests of any government to provoke conflict. Political globalisation further encourages dialogue between states and non-state actors over shared dilemmas, such as global terrorism and climate change.

Realists are globalisation-sceptics since they believe that the state is, and should remain, the main influence in international relations. Globalisation undermines the state's ability to protect the rights of its citizens and is also undemocratic since institutions of global governance lack a popular mandate. Since nation states act according to the best interests of their citizens, liberal attempts to encourage

Knowledge check 8

Explain why realists and liberals view globalisation so differently.

globalisation lack legitimacy and are potentially destabilising. As a result of this, realists are generally less ideologically committed to global free trade than liberals are, since they argue that the nation state should play a more positive role in developing national economic strategies and they doubt that all states benefit equally from economic globalisation. Realists are also sceptical about the extent to which liberal co-operation works in an anarchic world system. According to realism, Westphalian principles of state sovereignty provide the foundations for global stability. Therefore, liberal support for the United Nations, international law and regional integration will, at best, be ineffective and, at worst, encourage instability.

The debate between hyper-globalisers, globalisation sceptics and transformationalists

Hyper-globalisers

According to hyper-globalisers, globalisation has created a profound readjustment of global power that is challenging the centrality of the nation state. This is being achieved through free trade, instantaneous global communication and capital investment, the impact of influential non-state actors and the development of a more global culture. The growing need to resolve 'collective dilemmas' through international co-operation has also challenged state egoism as the main driver of policy. As a result, hyper-globalisers argue that an increasingly 'borderless' and 'post-sovereign state' world is being created. Nation states cannot insulate themselves from what is happening in the rest of the world and so a more interconnected global society and economy is continually being advanced. According to Philip Bobbitt, the nation state has thus been 'hollowed-out', creating a greater emphasis on **global governance**, which might eventually lead to some sort of **world government**.

Globalisation sceptics

Globalisation sceptics believe that the impact of globalisation has been greatly exaggerated. They argue that globalisation is not new. There have already been periods in history when world trade has greatly expanded, as it did during the late nineteenth century, while Europe, North Africa and the Middle East shared a much closer identity during the Roman period than they do today. Modern-day globalisation has also failed to really challenge state egoism as the main force influencing governments.

The failings of the Doha Round of World Trade Organization negotiations and the lack of authority of both the International Court of Justice (World Court) and the International Criminal Court demonstrates state egoism in action. The decision of the Trump administration to withdraw from the Trans-Pacific Partnership (TPP) and the Paris Climate Change Agreement in 2017 demonstrates the world's most influential state prioritising its own national interest. Brexit further illustrates the — perhaps surprising — resurgence of the nation state. Most trade still continues to happen within nation states. For example, the flow of finance, goods and services fell from a peak of 53 per cent of global output in 2007 to 39 per cent in 2014, highlighting the way in which enhanced economic globalisation is not necessarily inevitable.

Global governance refers to the way in which nation states no longer possess autonomy in decision-making and instead make collective decisions with other nation states and non-state actors through a variety of multilateral channels.

World government refers to the establishment of one sovereign and supranational body to which all the peoples and institutions across the world would be accountable. A world government would thus represent a world state and would possess supreme law-making powers.

Transformationalists

Transformationalists do not dispute that globalisation has had a profound impact on state sovereignty. They do disagree with hyper-globalisers over the future of the nation state, however. Instead of being rendered ultimately redundant by globalisation, states are adapting to the new realities it creates. For example, when states join regional organisations, such as the European Union, the North American Free Trade Agreement or the Association of Southeast Asian Nations, they do so in order to better advance their national interests, rather than as a way of ultimately abandoning their sovereignty.

Even though increasing economic and financial integration has raised the importance of transnational corporations (TNCs), states still determine their economic strategies in regard to the existing realities of the global economy. They are not simply depots through which international goods and capital flow. The way in which President Trump favours bilateral trade deals demonstrates how states can deploy globalisation to their advantage. China's importance as a nation state has been enhanced rather than diluted by the way in which it has exploited globalisation to its advantage.

Debates about the impact of globalisation, including its advantages and disadvantages

The impact of globalisation and its implications for the nation state and national sovereignty

Liberals argue that globalisation is bringing the world closer through trade, understanding and collective political endeavours. Not only does economic globalisation encourage greater global wealth and prosperity than ever before, it breaks down barriers between nation states and so encourages peace on the principle that, 'If goods do not cross borders, armies will.' The free exchange of ideas through the internet creates a global debate on issues such as climate change, and empowers individuals anywhere in the world to define their lives in ways that would have been unthinkable just a generation ago. Greater opportunities for nation states to co-operate with other nation states and non-state actors in institutions of global governance also create the potential one day for the sort of humane world government envisioned by Alfred Lord Tennyson in 'Locksley Hall' (1835):

> 'Till the war-drum throbb'd no longer, and the battle-flags were furl'd
>
> In the Parliament of man, the Federation of the world.
>
> There the common sense of most shall hold a fretful realm in awe,
>
> And the kindly earth shall slumber, lapt in universal law.'

Knowledge check 9

Explain the globalisation sceptic, hyper-globalisation and transformationalist interpretations of globalisation.

Others argue that this is a much too optimistic interpretation of globalisation and that its impact has often been highly destructive:

- According to dependency/world systems theory, economic globalisation enables the Global North to continue to exploit the Global South.
- Although economic globalisation has increased global wealth, it has drastically increased inequality within and between nation states, so contributing to both national and international tensions. Amy Chua makes this point powerfully in *World on Fire* (2002).
- The massive expansion of global trade is increasing carbon emissions through large-scale industrialisation and transportation, so endangering the sustainability of the planet.
- Cultural globalisation has created an unfulfilling obsession with materialism and has flattened out our valuable differences into a dull homogeneity based upon material fulfilment.
- Social media, rather than empowering us as individuals, contributes to depression and self-doubt.
- Instead of creating a global debate, instant communication creates an 'echo chamber', where prejudice is reinforced and nation states can advertise their nationalist world view globally (for example Russia Today, Fox News, Breitbart).
- The internet has provided terrorists with the opportunity to make converts globally.

How effectively does globalisation address and resolve contemporary problems?

Poverty

The extent to which globalisation reduces poverty is highly contentious. Free-market liberals argue that global prosperity is encouraged by expanding trade and providing new opportunities for investment. The neo-Marxist critique of Immanuel Wallerstein in world systems/dependency theory, however, suggests that economic globalisation enables core states to continue to dominate peripheral states by entrenching a neo-colonial world view.

Table 2 The debate over the impact of economic globalisation

'Globalisation conquers poverty'	'Globalisation increases poverty'
The reduction of tariffs encourages countries to trade more freely with each other, so creating more wealth.	TNCs open factories in the cheapest and least regulated economies, so creating 'a race to the bottom'.
Developing countries take advantage of new export opportunities, so leading to convergence between the Global North and Global South.	The developing world is swamped by cheap, mass-produced goods, so maintaining them in neo-colonial dependency (Wallerstein).
The expansion of global trade drives down the price of goods, so benefiting consumers everywhere.	Globalisation does not fairly distribute wealth, exacerbating the gap between rich and poor.

Conflict

Globalisation was initially expected to reduce conflict. According to the democratic peace thesis, by trading more freely with each other nation states would not go to war with each other, because this would mean mutually assured economic destruction.

Knowledge check 10

Why is economic globalisation so controversial?

Exam tip

When writing about the connection between globalisation and poverty and development, it is important that you also refer to the ideas covered in the section on Global governance: Economic (p.30).

Political globalisation would mean that more decisions would be negotiated through IGOs. In the immediate post-Cold War period, for example, there were several United Nations humanitarian interventions (Somalia, Bosnia and East Timor). As we have seen, in 2005 the UN World Summit endorsed Responsibility to Protect, which established the principle that the international community has a duty to intervene within states if human rights are being abused.

These high-minded ideals have been more honoured in the breach than the observance, however. Nation states have generally continued to put their own interests first, and so tragedies like the Rwandan genocide (1994) have been allowed to happen. The failure of the international community to work together to resolve the Syrian Civil War also demonstrates the failure of UN Responsibility to Protect to challenge Westphalian principles of non-intervention. Greater opportunities for the movement of people have often increased resentment and xenophobia, rather than liberal peace and harmony, as the free movement of the people within the European Union has illustrated.

Human rights

Although the Universal Declaration of Human Rights (1948) and a number of regional and UN courts and tribunals have been established to encourage and enforce a global standard of human rights, nation states remain the key arbiters of our human rights. As a result of this, international law remains simply soft law, which nation states often ignore if it conflicts with their interests:

- The principles of the UN Universal Declaration of Human Rights possess moral authority but are not binding on nation states, which determine the extent of the civil liberties of their citizens.
- The International Court of Justice (ICJ) or World Court requires the consent and co-operation of nation states if its judgements are to be enforced.
- Three of the five permanent members of the UN Security Council (Russia, China and the United States) have not joined the International Criminal Court (ICC) as they are not prepared to accept its jurisdiction.
- During the 2017 UK general election, Theresa May promised to change British human rights law if the European Convention on Human Rights gets 'in the way' of fighting terrorism.

Environment

In 2015, the UN Paris Climate Change Agreement achieved an almost total global consensus on the importance of the world working together to keep temperature increase during the twenty-first century 'well below' 2 degrees centigrade. This provides a good example of political globalisation, in which the world community came together to resolve a collective dilemma through a collective response. In 2017, however, the Trump administration declared that it would leave the agreement since it damaged the United States' immediate economic interests. According to President Trump, 'I was elected to represent the citizens of Pittsburgh, not Paris. I promised I would exit or re-negotiate any deal which fails to serve America's interests.' This, of course, demonstrates how national sovereignty and state egoism still hold back progress on climate change, as on so many other collective dilemmas.

Summary

When you have completed this topic you should have a thorough knowledge of the following information and issues:

- The meaning and significance of a nation state.
- The meaning and significance of globalisation.
- Ways in which globalisation has impacted the nation state.
- The difference between the realist and liberal views of globalisation.
- The meaning of, and differences between, the globalisation sceptic, hyper-globalisation and transformationalist interpretations of globalisation.
- The extent to which economic globalisation has reduced global poverty.
- The extent to which conflict is inevitable in global relations.
- The extent to which political globalisation successfully protects human rights and international law.

- The extent to which globalisation has led to a more collective global approach to the environment.

In addition, you should have gathered appropriate information to help you answer the following wide-ranging questions:

1 Examine the ways in which globalisation challenges the sovereignty of the nation state.
2 Evaluate the extent to which economic globalisation has had a greater impact than political globalisation.
3 Examine why globalisation is so controversial.
4 Evaluate the extent to which the nation state retains the central role in global politics.

Global governance: Political

The United Nations

Origins and development of the UN, including the 1945 UN Charter

The United Nations was established in 1945 in response to the global suffering caused by the Second World War. Its purpose, therefore, was to encourage greater co-operation between states in order to establish a system of global security that would resolve crises and encourage peace and development.

The United Nations' Charter clearly spells out its main aims:

- 'to save succeeding generations from the scourge of war' by encouraging the collective resolution of conflicts
- 'to reaffirm faith in fundamental human rights, in the dignity and worth of the human person, in the equal rights of men and women and of nations large and small'
- 'to ensure respect for international law'
- 'to promote social progress and better standards of life in larger freedom'

In 1948, the United Nations also published the Universal Declaration of Human Rights as a model for the rights that we may all claim by virtue of our common humanity.

The main governing organs of the United Nations are:

- The Security Council: The purpose of the Security Council is to enforce global peace and security. Fifteen nation states sit on the Security Council in New York, but only five of them (the United States, Russia, China, the United Kingdom and

The United Nations (UN) The world's most advanced intergovernmental organisation. It was established in 1945 and promotes peace, human rights, and social and economic development.

Security Council The main coercive body of the United Nations. Its five veto-wielding permanent members and ten rotating temporary members can pass legally binding resolutions in response to issues of conflict and security.

France) are permanent members that can wield the veto. The other ten members of the Security Council are not permanent and are elected for two-year terms. The Security Council passes binding resolutions that can impose economic sanctions, authorise peace-keeping missions and even approve military action against a nation state for aggression towards another member of the United Nations.

- The General Assembly: All 193 member states of the United Nations are members of the General Assembly, which also sits in New York. Each state has one vote and the General Assembly can debate any issue within the scope of the UN Charter. Some important issues — such as those connected with peace and security and agreeing the UN budget — require a two-thirds majority. General Assembly resolutions, however, unlike UN Security Council resolutions, are non-binding and so lack the force of international law. The General Assembly is, therefore, best seen as a deliberative rather than legislative body.

- The International Court of Justice: Also known as the World Court, the ICJ sits in The Hague, the Netherlands. Its 15 judges, elected by the General Assembly and Security Council for nine-year terms, arbitrate on cases submitted by nation states and can also deliver advisory opinions when submitted by UN agencies.

- The Economic and Social Council: The 54 members of the Economic and Social Council (ECOSOC) are elected by the General Assembly. Its role is to co-ordinate the social and economic work of United Nations' agencies, such as the World Health Organization (WHO), the United Nations High Commission for Refugees (UNHCR) and the United Nations Children's Fund (UNICEF). It also co-ordinates action with the International Monetary Fund, World Bank and World Trade Organization (the Bretton Woods Institutions).

The United Nations is thus a liberal institution of global governance that seeks to encourage co-operation between nation states, enhance international peace and security, and encourage development. Its influence is undermined, though, by the fact that global politics is still dominated by realist principles of state sovereignty. Thus, although Article 1 of the Charter of the United Nations commits the UN to maintaining 'international peace and security', Article 2 recognises 'the sovereign equality of all its Members'.

> **Exam tip**
>
> Contextualise references to the United Nations within the liberal–realist debate covered in the section on Theories of global politics (p.6). This will provide your writing with helpful theoretical insights.

The Security Council

The strengths and weaknesses of the Security Council are shown in Table 3.

Table 3 The strengths and weaknesses of the UN Security Council

Strengths	Weaknesses
By vesting the power of veto in the five permanent members of the Security Council, the UN is provided with clarity of leadership.	The right of the Permanent Five to wield the veto means that decisions to take military action need to be unanimous. Consequently, the Security Council has often failed to agree on military action.
Since its membership is so small, the Security Council can quickly be convened in response to an international crisis.	The membership of the Permanent Five represents the balance of world power in 1945 rather than today. This anachronism means that the interests of the emerging world are not sufficiently recognised by the Security Council. The legitimacy of the Security Council is thus questionable since it is not accountable to world opinion.

Strengths	Weaknesses
Requiring unanimity for military action ensures that the case for military action must be absolutely convincing. For example, in 2003 the UN Security Council was unconvinced by the Anglo-American case for war in Iraq and so refused to endorse military action.	The Security Council is unable to deploy a body of permanent standing troops. This means that even if it does agree on military action, by the time 'blue helmet' peace-keepers have been 'donated' by member states, many lives may already have been lost.
If the Security Council was further enlarged to include more veto-wielding states, it would be even more complicated to decide on military action.	

Why and in what ways could the UN Security Council be reformed?

Critics of the UN Security Council argue that it does not acknowledge the new realities of where power lies in global politics today. The power of veto of the Permanent Five also makes decision-making difficult. The lack of a permanently deployable military force further undermines its relevance. As former UN secretary-general Kofi Annan puts it, 'It is rather like telling the mayor [of New York]: we know you need a fire-house, but we'll build you one when the fire occurs.'

Potential reforms of the Security Council include:

- Emerging powers such as Brazil, India, Japan and Germany could be represented on the Security Council in order to provide it with contemporary legitimacy.
- By enlarging the membership of the Security Council, it would better represent global opinion.
- Voting on the Security Council could be by a qualified majority. Eliminating the veto would make it quicker and easier to implement military action in a security emergency.
- By establishing its own rapid reaction force, the Security Council would be able to intervene more quickly in emergencies.

The General Assembly

The strengths and weaknesses of the General Assembly are shown in Table 4.

Table 4 The strengths and weaknesses of the UN General Assembly

Strengths	Weaknesses
The General Assembly provides the only 'global forum' for multi-national debate of international issues. It is thus the closest we have yet come to a liberal institution of global governance or a 'parliament of nations'.	The General Assembly has been criticised for being a 'talk shop', which is irrelevant to pressing global issues.
The General Assembly is based upon the sovereign equality of all nation states, so each state has one vote. This means that, unlike in most institutions of global governance, such as the World Trade Organization, powerful states are not able to dominate less powerful states.	As well as being a strength, the equality of nation states on the General Assembly is also a weakness, because it means consensus is very hard to achieve.
By giving equal weight to the interests of all states, it enables even marginal powers to voice their opinions. Although its resolutions are non-binding, they do carry great weight because they are based upon the achievement of a truly global consensus. The General Assembly has, for example, played an important role in establishing a more *global* response to climate change.	Since its resolutions are non-binding and unenforceable, they can soon become irrelevant, which undermines the credibility of the General Assembly.

The International Court of Justice

The strengths and weaknesses of the International Court of Justice or World Court are shown in Table 5.

Table 5 The strengths and weaknesses of the International Court of Justice

Strengths	Weaknesses
The 15 judges of the ICJ represent the 'main forms of civilization and the principal legal systems of the world' (Article 9 of the ICJ statute). The ICJ is, therefore, the most advanced judicial organ for the implementation of international law and a key organ of liberal global governance.	The liberal principles of the ICJ conflict with realist 'state egoism'. According to realism, nation states seek to advance their own interests, which provides a strong incentive to ignore the rulings of the Court if they are not in a state's interests.
As such, it carries significant moral authority. Nation states do not want to be criticised by the ICJ, and as such it plays an important role in establishing a more 'rules-based' approach to conflict resolution.	Only 72 of the 193 members of the United Nations have agreed *in advance* to be bound by decisions of the ICJ, and even then the ICJ lacks the coercive power to enforce its will should they choose to ignore a judgement.
	The ICJ also cannot initiate cases. It can only provide judgements in cases that states present it with. When NGOs request its intervention the ICJ can simply present advisory opinions.

The Economic and Social Council

The strengths and weaknesses of the UN Economic and Social Council (ECOSOC) are shown in Table 6.

Table 6 The strengths and weaknesses of the UN Economic and Social Council

Strengths	Weaknesses
ECOSOC co-ordinates the work of a variety of aid agencies, each with a different focus on development.	ECOSOC has been accused of being bureaucratic and cumbersome. According to Helen Clark, who headed the UN Development Programme (UNDP) from 2009 to 2017, it has very little sense of strategic planning.
A major advantage of the ECOSOC is that it has advanced the principle that development should not be measured simply in economic terms. Instead, 'human development' needs to be understood much more broadly.	ECOSOC has also been accused of being fragmented, with different agencies fulfilling the same role and competing for the same resources.
ECOSOC thus administers a growing number of agencies that address different challenges. These include the UN's Environment Programme, the Office of the UN High Commissioner for Refugees (UNHCR), the UN Human Rights Council (UNHRC) and the UN Children's Fund (UNICEF). The UN Development Programme (UNDP) co-ordinates development programmes in 177 nation states and since 1990 has published Human Development reports.	The large number of development agencies that operate in one country also means that their jurisdiction overlaps so much that accountability is blurred and delivery impeded.
ECOSOC has also given development greater global significance by establishing and publicising global targets such as the Millennium Development Goals (2000–15) and the Sustainable Development Goals (2015–30).	Important roles within ECOSOC are determined less on merit than on ensuring that all states feel adequately represented. Saudi Arabia, for example, which has a highly controversial record on human rights, sits on the Human Rights Council because no other country competed for its seat.

How effectively does the United Nations Security Council resolve conflict?

When the Security Council agrees to work together, it can achieve peace-making success. In 1990, for example, it mandated military action to evict Iraqi forces from Kuwait and then authorised the establishment of UN safe havens within Iraq in 1991 to limit Saddam Hussein's aggression towards his own citizens.

The United Nations has also mandated effective peace-keeping 'blue helmet' missions in East Timor and Côte d'Ivoire, which have been well resourced and proactive.

The effectiveness of the UN is undermined, however, because its liberal intentions conflict with the realist self-interest of nation states:

- The Permanent Five often put their own strategic interests first on the Security Council and so fail to agree on military intervention. This is why the Rwandan genocide was not prevented in 1994 and why there has been no UN intervention in Syria since its civil war began in 2011.
- UN peace-keeping missions have often been under-resourced and have lacked a sufficiently 'robust' mandate to enforce peace. They can thus end up being marginalised. This happened during the Bosnian Civil War (1991–95) and more recently in the Democratic Republic of the Congo and Darfur.

Knowledge check 11

What are the main functions of the United Nations?

How effectively does the United Nations address poverty?

The United Nations plays an important role in reducing poverty, protecting the vulnerable and encouraging development. The Economic and Social Committee (ECOSOC) co-ordinates the work of regional development councils and significant development agencies, including:

- the World Health Organization (WHO)
- the United Nations Children's Fund (UNICEF)
- the United Nations Development Programme (UNDP)
- the World Bank and the International Monetary Fund (IMF)

Knowledge check 12

In what ways does the United Nations address the problem of poverty?

The UN's Millennium Development Goals (2000–15) and Sustainable Development Goals (2015–30) have also provided important global targets in the reduction of global poverty, as well as in the way in which poverty needs to be addressed in both economic and non-economic ways.

Critics point out that UN aid agencies often overlap and that performance is poorly monitored. World systems theory also suggests that the IMF and World Bank are actually reinforcing structural inequalities.

How effectively does the United Nations protect human rights?

The United Nations Universal Declaration of Human Rights (1948) establishes a moral goal that nation states should aspire to. A number of UN tribunals (the former Yugoslavia, Rwanda, Sierra Leone and Cambodia) have also prosecuted war crimes, and in 2002 the International Criminal Court was established under the auspices of the UN to try individuals accused of war crimes and crimes against humanity. In 2005 the UN's World Summit issued 'Responsibility to Protect', which inaugurated the principle that the international community has the *responsibility* to intervene within nation states in order to stop mass murder, torture or preventable loss of life.

What the UN can do to enforce respect for human rights, though, is severely limited by realism and sovereignty. Because of this, states often put their own self-interest above that of international law, in addition to which the UN lacks the means to enforce its principles.

- The Universal Declaration of Human Rights is a form of non-binding soft law that nation states are free to ignore.
- The International Criminal Court requires the consent of nation states to be effective. Three members of the UN Security Council (Russia, China and the United States) refuse to accept its jurisdiction, since it challenges their state sovereignty.
- UN Responsibility to Protect has been widely ignored, notably over Syria, because it conflicts with the Westphalian principle of state sovereignty, which realists argue is vital for the maintenance of global stability.

How effectively does the United Nations address environmental issues?

The United Nations has been very successful in highlighting the problem of climate change. The reports of the United Nations' Intergovernmental Panel on Climate Change have focused global attention on the potentially devastating cost of climate change. UN summits on climate change (Kyoto 1997, Copenhagen 2009, and Paris 2015) have also established a growing consensus among countries that an international response to the problem is required.

As with human rights protection and conflict resolution, the ability of the UN to protect the environment is hampered by the fact that nation states cannot be forced to cut their carbon emissions. The UN can thus set targets, such as keeping temperature rise in the twenty-first century below 2 degrees centigrade, but if states renege on their commitments, or fail to make them, then that is their choice.

North Atlantic Treaty Organization

To what extent has NATO's role changed since the end of the Cold War?

The North Atlantic Treaty Organization was established in 1949 in order to protect the West from possible Soviet aggression. This was done by establishing the principle of collective security (Article 5), whereby an attack on one member would provoke a military response by the whole of NATO. Such a combined response would thus deter Soviet expansionism.

During the Cold War, NATO thus provided Western Europe with military protection. Its defensive nature meant that it was able to do this without firing a shot. When the Soviet Union collapsed in 1991 and the Cold War ended, however, NATO's necessity began to be questioned. In order to maintain its significance, its role began to change on the principle of 'out of area or out of existence'.

Knowledge check 13

How does realism relate to the difficulties the United Nations has in achieving its objectives?

The North Atlantic Treaty Organization (NATO) NATO was established in 1949 to provide 12 Western countries with collective security (Article 5) against potential Soviet aggression. By 2017 NATO's membership had risen to 29 and it continues to provide security for its members, on the principle that an attack on one member will trigger a collective response by all.

Increasingly, NATO's role was interpreted as requiring proactive operations in conflicts that, if not resolved, could threaten Western security. These operations have ranged from Europe to Afghanistan to Africa:

■ In 1995 NATO intervened in the Bosnian Civil War, bombing Bosnian Serb positions. This established the conditions for the subsequent signing of the Dayton Peace Accords (1995).

■ In 1999 NATO bombed Serbia in order to stop the government's military offensives within Kosovo.

■ In both Bosnia and Kosovo, NATO subsequently played an important role in 'nation-building' once the fighting had stopped.

■ From 2001 to 2014 NATO's International Security Assistance Force (ISAF) played a major role in supporting Afghan forces against Taliban insurgency. Since 2015 its successor, Operation Resolute Support, has trained and advised Afghan forces in their continuing struggle to expand the government's authority.

■ In 2011 NATO intervened in Libya to implement UN Resolution 1973, stopping the government's attacks on civilians. As a result of its military action the Gaddafi regime was overthrown.

■ From 2009 to 2016 NATO's Operation Ocean Shield combatted piracy in the Indian Ocean.

> **Knowledge check 14**
>
> In what ways has NATO's role changed since its foundation in 1949?

Although NATO has acted significantly out of area in recent years, this is not to say it has abandoned its original purpose:

■ Since the end of the Cold War NATO has expanded far into Eastern Europe. Its newer members, such as the Baltic States (Latvia, Lithuania and Estonia) and Poland, are acutely conscious of the importance of 'collective security' in protecting their independence.

■ Under President Putin, Russia has become more assertive. In 2008 Russia attacked Georgia in support of South Ossetia's claims for independence, and in 2014 Russia annexed Crimea from Ukraine. This indicates how vulnerable Russia's non-NATO neighbours are and has reinforced the importance of 'collective security' in deterring the possibility of further Russian expansionism.

■ The failure of NATO to bring stability to Afghanistan and Libya has reinforced the belief that NATO has tried to do 'too much' and should return to its original focus.

Strengths of NATO

■ A major success of NATO has been to maintain the strong military relationship between the United States and Western Europe. This has made it less likely that the United States could become isolationist, undermining European security.

■ By expanding its reach into Eastern Europe, NATO is providing security guarantees to new democracies and reducing the risk of a Russian 'divide and conquer' strategy.

■ Defensive realists, like Kenneth Waltz, argue that NATO encourages peace by providing incentives for Russia not to threaten Western interests.

■ NATO's new 'Very High Readiness Joint Task Force' (VJTF) is extremely flexible and adaptable in an emergency.

- NATO recognises the way in which threats to Western interests are 'multi-directional' and that it must present a united front against new challenges such as Islamist terrorism.

Weaknesses of NATO

- By expanding to 29 member states (2017), NATO now has to provide 'collective security' to states very close to Russia's zone of influence. This could undermine Article 5, which focuses on a direct military attack on a member of NATO, since not all member states may feel equally prepared to provide collective security if Russia threatened its more vulnerable neighbours. By becoming so big, is NATO's sense of solidarity being undermined?
- The United States has complained that too many states 'freeload' off NATO. Only four European members of NATO spend more than 2 per cent of their GDP on defence (a NATO recommendation), and yet they still claim the benefits of collective security.
- The commitment of some members, like Turkey and Hungary, to collective security has been questioned.
- Advances in cyber technology may be the aggression of the future. Whether this would lead to the triggering of Article 5 is less certain.
- NATO's primary role in the protection of Western Europe could also be diluted by Jean-Claude Juncker's plans for a European army.

> **Knowledge check 15**
>
> In what ways has NATO been criticised?

Summary

When you have completed this topic you should have a thorough knowledge of the following information and issues:

- The main principles of the United Nations' Charter (1945).
- The purpose of the UN Security Council.
- The strengths and weaknesses of the UN Security Council.
- Why and how the UN Security Council could be reformed.
- The main functions of the UN General Assembly.
- The strengths and weaknesses of the UN General Assembly.
- The main functions of the International Court of Justice.
- Factors undermining the effectiveness of the International Court of Justice.
- The main functions of the Economic and Social Council (ECOSOC).
- Criticisms of the Economic and Social Council.
- Examples of UN peace-keeping and peace-making operations.
- How effective the United Nations is in resolving conflict.

- How effective the United Nations is in combatting poverty and advancing development.
- How effective the United Nations is in protecting human rights.
- The significance of the United Nations in protecting the environment.
- The reasons why the North Atlantic Treaty Organization (NATO) was established in 1949.
- Examples of NATO's peace-making missions.
- The extent to which the role of NATO has changed since the end of the Cold War.
- The strengths and weaknesses of NATO.

In addition, you should have gathered appropriate information to help you answer the following wide-ranging questions:

1 Examine the factors that undermine the effectiveness of the United Nations.
2 Evaluate the extent to which the United Nations is a successful organisation.
3 Examine the reasons why it has been difficult to achieve reform of the UN Security Council.
4 Evaluate the extent to which NATO has returned to its original purpose.

■ Global governance: Economic

Role and significance of the International Monetary Fund and the World Bank

In 1944, towards the end of the Second World War, 44 nation states met at Bretton Woods in New Hampshire to establish the principles by which the post-war global economy would be organised. Economists and politicians were acutely aware of how the Wall Street Crash (1929) had provoked global economic nationalism as states erected trade barriers (tariffs) against each other. This had, in turn, stimulated aggressive nationalism, which had led to the outbreak of war in 1939.

A new system of global economic governance was thus needed that would maintain global economic stability and encourage economic development, so ensuring peace and security. The first two pillars of what became known as the Bretton Woods system were the International Monetary Fund and the World Bank.

The International Monetary Fund

As of 2017, 189 nation states are members of the **International Monetary Fund**. It encourages global financial stability in three main ways:

1　The IMF monitors the economic health and stability of its members and warns against policies that it considers could be damaging to that economy. This is known as surveillance. For example, the IMF has advised Mexico that it is too dependent on oil revenue and that it should, therefore, diversify in order to cushion its economy in case of a drop in the price of oil.

2　The IMF also offers technical advice to countries on how best to maximise their economic potential. For example, in Peru the IMF has been advising the government on improving its methods of tax collection.

3　The IMF acts as a lender of last resort. If a member country is facing a balance of payments crisis then it can access emergency loans through requesting special drawing rights. This should stabilise its currency and save the country from possible bankruptcy, so ensuring that the contagion does not spread elsewhere which could potentially cause a global economic crisis. IMF loans are generally 'conditional' on the recipient country undergoing free-market **structural adjustment programmes** in order to resolve the problems that had caused its economy to come so close to collapse. Structural adjustment programmes can include the imposition of reforms, such as cuts in public spending, privatisation, reductions in tariffs and subsidies, and devaluation of the currency (in order to encourage exports).

IMF successes

According to neo-liberal supporters of the Washington Consensus, the International Monetary Fund is vital in encouraging economic stability and development:

■ Global free trade is encouraged by discouraging nation states from adopting tariffs, so maximising global wealth.

International Monetary Fund (IMF) The International Monetary Fund was established in 1945 following the Bretton Woods Conference. It is designed to ensure global financial stability by providing loans to countries facing a balance of payments crisis, encouraging free trade/free markets and monitoring economic performance.

Structural adjustment programme (SAP) In return for loans, both the International Monetary Fund and the World Bank can require recipient states to introduce structural adjustment programmes. These generally involve the imposition of free-market reforms, which is why the loans are said to be conditional.

- By encouraging free-market reforms, nation states are more able to take advantage of the opportunities offered by economic globalisation.
- Like the World Bank, the International Monetary Fund has encouraged debt relief for developing countries that are introducing free-market reforms. In 2015, for example, the IMF granted Chad, the fourth-poorest country in the world, $1.1 billion in debt relief.
- As a lender of last resort, the IMF provides the global economy with greater stability, since if a nation state is facing severe economic problems the international community knows it can access emergency loans. This certainty provides the global economy with a greater sense of confidence, so reducing the risk of a collective panic that could in turn provoke a global depression.

By adopting IMF-inspired reforms, a number of countries have been able to develop much stronger free-market economies:

- IMF SAPs in India in the 1990s encouraged the country to diversify from agriculture into new growth sectors, such as the service industry.
- IMF SAPs in Africa have encouraged it to diversify from subsistence agriculture into world markets, so significantly boosting growth rates in the continent.

IMF emergency loans have also been vital in maintaining global stability in times of economic crisis. Such a 'crisis firewall' has encouraged states to keep on trading and investing, so restoring global confidence:

- In 1997 the South Korean economy was rescued with a $55 billion aid package.
- During the 2008 global financial crisis, the IMF provided emergency loans to vulnerable economies such as Hungary, Romania and Ukraine. Without such loans, these countries could have faced bankruptcy. The resulting contagion as they defaulted on their global creditors would have made the financial crash even worse.
- Since the euro sovereign debt crisis began in 2009, the IMF and the European Central Bank have made extensive loans to Greece in order to restore confidence in its economy. By doing this, the risk of other vulnerable European economies — such as Portugal, Italy and Spain — being undermined has been reduced, so averting a pan-European economic crisis.
- In total, from 2008 to 2016, the IMF committed $700 billion to its member countries in order to maintain trust in the global economy.

Criticisms of the IMF

- A major criticism of the International Monetary Fund is that it represents solely the neo-liberal Western-oriented approach to economic development. Economists like Jeffrey Sachs and Joseph Stiglitz thus criticise the free-market 'one size fits all' mentality of the IMF.
- IMF SAPs have been accused of undermining already-fragile economies, so that free-market 'shock therapy' actually ends up killing the patient.
- SAPs are also accused of undermining national sovereignty since desperate states, like Greece, may have no alternative but to accept the conditions of their loans.
- The president of the IMF is by convention always a European (Christine Lagarde since 2011). Also, the United States possesses 16.74 per cent of the votes on the IMF and, since an 85 per cent vote is required to change its constitution, the United States has an effective veto over the way in which the IMF does business.

Knowledge check 16

What are the main functions of the International Monetary Fund?

■ The IMF has been accused of failing in its task of surveillance since it was taken by surprise by both the global financial crisis and the euro sovereign debt crisis.

The World Bank

The focus of the **World Bank** is on long-term development. It is made up of the International Bank for Reconstruction and Development (IBRD), which makes loans to middle-income countries, and the International Development Agency, which makes loans to the poorest countries in the world.

Especially since the 1990s, the World Bank's loans have required recipient states to carry through extensive free-market SAPs. According to the neo-liberal economic principles of the World Bank, this is because the developing world can only achieve long-term prosperity by embracing globalisation.

World Bank successes

■ By encouraging diversification away from subsistence agriculture through SAPs, developing countries have been able to take advantage of new opportunities in the global economy. This has helped to encourage growing convergence between the economies of the Global North and the Global South.

■ The World Bank has also taken the lead in encouraging debt relief for developing countries through the Highly Indebted Poor Countries Initiative.

■ In addition to being a 'money bank' the World Bank is also a 'knowledge bank', and under recent presidents (Robert Zoellick 2007–12 and Jim Kim 2012–) it has increasingly focused on developing human resources by investing in education, business training, gender-equality schemes and fighting diseases like AIDS. It is also playing a major role in combatting climate change, measuring its projects in terms of environmental sustainability.

■ Recent World Bank projects have increasingly focused on 'country ownership', providing recipient states with a greater say over how the loans are spent.

Criticisms of the World Bank

The World Bank can be criticised for its belief that the imposition of free markets on the developing world is the best way of achieving economic growth.

■ According to Immanuel Wallerstein's world systems theory, the Washington Consensus maintains developing economies in a peripheral/subordinate status. This is because when they open up their markets to foreign competition, the developed world 'dumps' cheap mass-produced products on them, so ensuring that they remain in a state of dependency.

■ Opening up markets to global competition undermines traditional industries and small-scale farming. The resulting unemployment can lead to a significant increase in social problems.

■ Structural adjustment programmes often require developing countries to dramatically cut public spending. This can have a devastating impact on their already poor populations.

■ Conditionality infringes on the sovereign right of nation states to determine their own economic policies.

World Bank was founded in 1945 as a result of the Bretton Woods Conference. It provides long-term loans and support, training and advice to developing countries.

Knowledge check 17

In what ways does the World Bank encourage development?

Role and significance of the World Trade Organization, G7/G8 and G20

The World Trade Organization

The World Trade Organization was established in 1995 and, together with the International Monetary Fund and World Bank, comprises the Bretton Woods system of global economic governance. The WTO aims to expand global trade by encouraging its member states to reduce tariffs and subsidies. This is done on the 'most favoured nation' principle, so that if you grant special trading favours to one member of the WTO then they must also be granted to all members. Various trade rounds focus on reducing tariffs in specific areas.

As well as establishing the rules by which nation states trade with each other, the WTO also negotiates trade disputes between countries. By 2017, the WTO had 164 members. Significantly, China became a member of the WTO in 2001 and Russia in 2012.

World Trade Organization (WTO) is the successor to the General Agreement on Trade and Tariffs. It was established in 1995 and is designed to increase world trade by encouraging member states to reduce tariffs and settle trade disputes.

World Trade Organization successes

- By discouraging tariffs and subsidies, the WTO has helped to dramatically expand global trade. This has created greater global prosperity and helped to reduce global poverty (see Table 7).

Table 7 Values of global trade 1950–2013

Value of global trade (1950)	$296 billion
Value of global trade (2005)	$8 trillion
Value of global trade (2013)	$18.8 trillion

- The WTO has resolved a number of trade disputes between its members, so encouraging a 'rules-based' approach to global conflict.
- In spite of the 2008 global economic crash, WTO members did not resort to tariff protectionism, which would have extended the recession and encouraged dangerous resentment between states.
- According to the democratic peace thesis, by encouraging free trade, the WTO reduces the risk of conflict.

Criticisms of the World Trade Organization

- The WTO is solely concerned with expanding global trade. It does not address related problems such as the impact on workers' rights, child labour, environmental degradation or sustainability.
- Powerful lobbying groups from the developed world exert too much influence at WTO headquarters in Geneva.
- By encouraging developing countries to open up their markets to foreign competition, the WTO is undermining their potential for growth. The Doha Trade Round (2001–) has been so ineffective because developing countries have not been prepared to open their markets to cheaply produced agricultural produce from the developed world.

Knowledge check 18

Why is the World Trade Organization controversial?

The G7/G8 and G20

The **G7/G8** and the **G20** enable leaders of the most powerful economies in the world to meet on a regular basis to discuss global issues. The G7 is restricted to the most powerful economies in the Global North. Russia also became a member in 1997, making it the G8, but was suspended in 2014 following the annexation of Crimea. In 2017 Russia signalled its intention of permanently leaving the body because it is so unrepresentative of contemporary global economic influence. In contrast, the G20 comprises the most powerful economies in both the Global North and the Global South.

G7 and G20 successes

- By providing a regular point of contact for the world's most powerful countries, the G7 and G20 encourage global trust and co-operation.
- The G7 and G20 enable member states to co-ordinate action on 'collective dilemmas', such as the global economy, climate change, terrorism and weapons of mass destruction.
- In 2009, members of the G20 memorably agreed not to respond to the global economic crisis by adopting protectionist 'beggar thy neighbour' strategies.

Criticisms of the G7 and G20

- The G7 has been criticised for reinforcing the Global North–South divide and also for being unnecessary since the establishment of the G20. Since it is so unrepresentative its legitimacy has been questioned.
- The membership of the G20 has also been criticised for being arbitrary. Argentina is a member but not Spain, which has a bigger economy.
- The exclusive membership of both undermines what should be inclusive economic global governance.
- Both the G7 and G20 have been criticised for not being able to bind their members to agreements. They issue only declarations of intent and so have been accused of being expensive 'talk shops'.

How effectively does global economic governance deal with poverty?

The North–South divide

The term **North–South divide** was first used in the Brandt Reports in 1980 and 1983 and highlights the economic and social divisions between the developed (the Global North) and the developing (the Global South) worlds. According to this terminology:

- The Global North is more industrially developed and prosperous than the Global South, which is poorer and more focused on agricultural production.
- The Global North dominates investment, enterprise and innovation.
- Transnational corporations are generally based in the Global North.
- Overseas aid goes from the Global North to the Global South.
- Foreign direct investment generally goes from the Global North to the Global South.
- Governments in the Global North are more likely to be democratic and to respect human rights, and endemic corruption is more likely in the Global South.

G7/G8 and **G20** The G7, or Group of Seven, comprises the seven most powerful economies in the Global North. The G20, or Group of Twenty, is an international forum for the leaders of the world's biggest economies. Its members come from both the Global North and the Global South.

North–South divide contrasts the industrialisation and prosperity of the Global North with the poorer and more agricultural Global South. It is best understood as a political rather than a geographical term.

- Governments in the Global North are more stable, and civil disorder is more likely in the Global South.

Growing 'convergence' between the economies of the Global North and the Global South has led to the term being criticised as anachronistic and stereotypical. It is still used to denote those ways in which there are still major structural disparities between the developed and developing worlds, however.

Neo-classical development theory

Since the end of the Cold War in 1991, neo-classical development theory has dominated the main principles of economic global governance. Neo-classical development theory is closely associated with the eighteenth-century economist Adam Smith, who argued that free markets and free trade provide the 'invisible hand' that benefits everyone in society. Attempts by governments to protect or regulate trade undermine economic growth by discouraging enterprise, initiative and innovation.

The International Monetary Fund, the World Bank and the World Trade Organization are collectively known as the Bretton Woods Institutions. As organs of global economic governance, they collectively encourage the adoption of free-market neo-classical development theories. This is sometimes referred to as 'economic globalisation' or the 'Washington Consensus'.

Dependency and world systems theory

Hans Singer and Raúl Prebisch developed **dependency theory** in the 1940s. They argued that developing countries can escape dependency on developed countries only by protecting themselves from their cheap exports.

This theory was further developed by Immanuel Wallerstein in the 1970s in his neo-Marxist world systems theory. According to Wallerstein, economic liberalism is used by the developed world to maintain its neo-colonial dominance over peripheral states:

- Free trade allows core states to 'dump' cheap manufactured products on peripheral states. Developing countries are thus so dependent on the cheap imports that they have no incentive to establish their own manufacturing base. They therefore fail to reach a proto-industrial stage of development.
- Core states also utilise the opening up of markets to exploit the developing world's cheap workforce.
- The developing world's raw materials are also exploited by core states, further entrenching their economic dominance.
- The profits of economic globalisation thus continue to be reaped in the Global North as the Global South is locked into a subordinate role in the global economy.

Structural theory

World systems and dependency theory suggests that economic liberalism builds in structural inequalities into international relations. The encouragement of free markets has thus been criticised as neo-colonialism. In order to protect the developing world from exploitation, structural theory therefore recommends that the developing world protects itself from exploitation and builds up its economic potential to a level where it can compete more fairly with the developed world. The Cambridge economist Ha Joon Chang, for example, has strongly criticised neo-classical development theory, arguing that

Dependency theory
According to this theory, by encouraging free trade, wealthy (Global North) countries are able to exploit poorer (Global South) countries by making them dependent on their cheap mass-produced goods.

Knowledge check 19

In what ways does world systems/ dependency theory challenge neo-classical economic theory?

developing states should provide tariff protection and subsidies for their infant industries so that they develop to a level where they can fairly compete in the global economy.

Orthodox and alternative measurements of poverty

The orthodox approach to development has been to measure it in economic terms. Therefore, the emphasis of development has been to reduce poverty through increasing the wage-earning potential of people in the developing world. The World Bank currently defines poverty as living on less than $1.90 a day, and development economics has thus focused on raising living standards by raising income levels.

Alternative measurements of poverty and development acknowledge that human happiness is not based solely upon material well-being. Indeed, economic development can bring with it its own problems, such as growing inequality, social breakdown, consumerism and insecurity. Therefore, alternative models of development focus on poverty reduction in much broader, non-economic terms. These include ensuring:

- that economic development is compatible with the protection of human rights
- that the living conditions and employment rights of workers are protected
- that industrialisation does not threaten the environment, and that economic development is measured in terms of its impact on the environment
- that women's rights are protected and that gender equality is encouraged
- that wealthier societies should not be allowed to become so unequal that social cohesion and inclusivity is threatened
- that greater consumerism does not degenerate into pure materialism, so subsuming diverse cultures within global cultural homogeneity

Knowledge check 20

What are the main differences between the orthodox and alternative models of development?

In what ways could global economic governance be reformed?

Critics of global economic governance argue that it is too based on neo-classical development theory and the interests of the Global North. This means that it focuses too much on free markets and global wealth creation, without appreciating enough the diverse requirements of different states and the importance of regulating capital movements. The following reforms have thus been suggested:

- The International Monetary Fund (IMF) should be able to provide some regulation of international capital movements, so that the global financial crisis of 2007–09 is not repeated.
- The Global South should have greater voting influence on both the World Bank and the IMF, so its interests are better represented.
- The presidencies of the Bretton Woods Institutions should not be confined to the Global North.
- Recipient states should have greater influence over the requirements of World Bank and IMF structural adjustment programmes.
- The question of whether free markets can threaten development should be addressed, rather than always assuming that all states benefit equally from free markets.
- The Bretton Woods Institutions should focus more on alternative forms of development that pay greater attention to human capital and sustainability.

Exam tip

When examining the effectiveness of global economic governance, contextualise your answers within the neo-Marxist and neo-classical traditions.

The role and significance of the global civil society and non-state actors, including non-governmental organisations, in encouraging development

In addition to intergovernmental organs of global economic governance, non-governmental organisations play a major role in encouraging development. These include:

- the Red Cross
- Oxfam
- Christian Aid
- the Gates Foundation
- the Carter Foundation

Dambisa Moyo in *Dead Aid*, however, has questioned the effectiveness of international aid, arguing that it discourages entrepreneurship, initiative and good governance, and instead encourages corruption and unhelpful stereotypical attitudes towards the developing world. Blamed by some for encouraging a 'white saviour complex' in the developing world, journalist Mark Steyn has warned that the good intentions of NGOs risk making Africa 'the permanent poster child for the world's irredeemable losers'.

Non-governmental organisations (NGOs) Private not-for-profit organisations that seek to improve global society and the environment. NGOs, like Friends of the Earth or Save the Children, thus work with nation states and intergovernmental organisations in order to achieve their philanthropic objectives.

Summary

When you have completed this topic you should have a thorough knowledge of the following information and issues:

- What the main features of the neo-classical approach to economic development are.
- Why the International Monetary Fund was established.
- The successes and failures of the International Monetary Fund.
- What the aims of the World Bank are.
- Why the World Bank is so controversial.
- The purpose of structural adjustment programmes and why they are controversial.
- What the aims of the World Trade Organization are.
- The successes and failures of the World Trade Organization.
- The main criticisms of the Bretton Woods Institutions.
- A comparison between the membership of the G7(8) and G20.
- The aims of the G7(8) and the G20, and ways in which they have both been criticised.

- The world systems or dependency theory criticism of economic globalisation.
- The meaning of 'neo-colonialism' and how it relates to dependency theory.
- A comparison between orthodox and alternative approaches to poverty and development.
- Ways in which global economic governance could be reformed.

In addition, you should have gathered appropriate information to help you answer the following wide-ranging questions:

1 Examine how effective the Bretton Woods Institutions are in encouraging economic growth and stability.
2 Evaluate the extent to which economic globalisation can conquer poverty and bring prosperity to all.
3 Examine why there is such tension between the orthodox and alternative approaches to poverty and development.
4 Evaluate the extent to which global economic governance is in need of *urgent* reform.

■ Global governance: Human rights

Origins and development of international law

The United Nations was established in 1945 as a liberal organ of global governance that would protect the rights of nation states *and* of human beings from abuse and exploitation. The rise of aggressive nationalism during the 1930s, which had culminated in global war and genocide, demonstrated that nation states could not be relied upon to protect the rights of their citizens or to live in harmony with each other. Therefore, the United Nations would provide new safeguards that would create a more harmonious world based upon tolerance, respect and security.

Sources of authority

1 The Charter of the United Nations (1945) established the International Court of Justice (ICJ) to settle disputes between nation states and provide advisory opinions on legal questions. As a result of this a more stable global society could be established, in which strong states would no longer be able to exploit their power by the use of force.

2 The way in which Nazi Germany and Japan had systematically abused the rights of racial and ethnic groups also made it important to define a **universal** standard of **human rights**. The United Nations' Universal Declaration of Human Rights (1948) was thus drawn up to enshrine human rights in one, universally applicable, document.

The Universal Declaration of Human Rights

In 1948, the United Nations published the Universal Declaration of Human Rights, which establishes the absolute civil, political and social freedoms that all humans enjoy. It is based upon 'the inherent dignity' of all human beings and defines 'the equal and inalienable rights of all members of the human family'. It is not a legally enforceable document, but possesses great moral force as a summary of the standards of human rights to which nation states should aspire.

> **Universal human rights** The rights that all human beings have by virtue of their humanity. They cannot be qualified or limited and apply to all humans irrespective of gender, sexual orientation, nationality, race or religion.

The International Court of Justice

The **International Court of Justice** is a liberal institution of global governance that provides the opportunity for nation states to resolve their differences through international arbitration:

■ A ruling by the ICJ carries considerable moral weight and so nation states will not want to be in defiance of the Court.

■ Non-compliance by a state with an ICJ judgement means that the other party may then approach the UN Security Council to enforce the judgement.

To be effective, however, the rule of law needs to be enforceable and all states should be held equally accountable for their actions. This is not the case with the ICJ because:

■ it cannot initiate cases itself

> **International Court of Justice (ICJ)** The International Court of Justice, or World Court, is the United Nations' primary judicial branch. Established by the UN Charter in 1945, it sits in The Hague and is designed to settle disputes between nation states.

- if states choose to ignore judgements or rulings by the Court, it is highly unlikely that the UN Security Council will take coercive action

The success of the ICJ thus primarily depends upon states being prepared to accept its decisions. By 2017, only 72 of the 193 members of the Court had signed the optional clause that means they agree in advance to agree to the rulings of the Court.

In addition to its judgements, the ICJ can also be asked by non-state actors to provide advisory opinions. As these are non-binding, their relevance is severely limited.

Table 8 examines whether the ICJ is effective in promoting respect for international law.

Knowledge check 21

What are the main limitations on the effectiveness of the International Court of Justice (World Court)?

Table 8 Is the International Court of Justice effective in promoting respect for international law?

Yes	No
The ICJ possesses great moral authority and on a number of occasions states have agreed to accept its rulings.	The ICJ lacks coercive power and so its judgements and opinions require the co-operation of states if they are to be enforced.
1986: Border clash between Burkina Faso and Mali was resolved.	1980: Iran refused to acknowledge the sovereignty of the ICJ when the USA accused it of breaking international law by seizing the American embassy in Tehran in 1979.
1992: Border dispute between Honduras and El Salvador was resolved.	1984: The ICJ declared that the Reagan administration had acted illegally by mining Nicaraguan harbours in order to topple the Sandinista government. The United States refused to accept the judgement, arguing that its actions were a justifiable response to Nicaraguan threats to its neighbours.
2002: Border dispute between Nigeria and Cameroon was resolved.	2004: Israel rejected the ICJ's opinion that the wall it was building to separate Israel from the Palestinian territories was illegal.

The European Court of Human Rights

The Council of Europe was established in 1949 and is responsible for promoting human rights and the rule of law in Europe. In 1950 it passed the European Convention on Human Rights, which defines the rights of European citizens. The European Court of Human Rights sits in Strasbourg and hears cases involving breaches of the European Convention.

Table 9 examines whether the European Court of Human Rights is effective.

Table 9 Is the European Court of Human Rights effective?

Yes	No
All European states, excluding Belarus, are members of the Council and so are members of the European Convention on Human Rights.	Like the ICJ and ICC, the European Court of Human Rights lacks coercive authority.
Judgements of the European Court of Human Rights possess great moral authority.	The UK government has failed to comply with a number of its rulings, such as the prohibition of prisoner voting being in defiance of the Convention.
Member states do not want to be seen to be in defiance of a ruling of the Court. Compliance with its judgements is 90 per cent.	Russia has declared that its national law takes precedence over the European Convention.

United Nations tribunals

As a result of the greater centrality of human rights in international relations, the United Nations Security Council established four war crimes tribunals in response to the extensive human rights abuses that had taken place in Cambodia in the 1970s and in the former Yugoslavia, Sierra Leone and Rwanda in the 1990s.

The aims of these **United Nations tribunals** have been to:

- bring to justice the perpetrators of these crimes
- develop the principle that heads of government can be held accountable for atrocities
- expose the horrors of these crimes against humanity in order to stop them being repeated
- establish the principle of a global community that will not tolerate such human rights abuses

United Nations tribunals Four United Nations international tribunals have been established since the 1990s, to prosecute those responsible for crimes against humanity in the former Yugoslavia, Cambodia, Sierra Leone and Rwanda.

Table 10 Successes of the United Nations tribunals

Tribunal	Successes
Former Yugoslavia (1993)	By 2017, the tribunal had convicted and sentenced 83 war criminals. Leading political and military figures, such as Bosnian Serb leader Radovan Karadžić, have been punished for their crimes (Karadžić was sentenced to 40 years). The last case to be heard is that of the Bosnian Serb military commander, Ratko Mladić. The detail of atrocities such as Srebrenica (1995) have been made public, making it harder to deny them. The principle that heads of state can be legally held accountable for the actions of their government was established when Serbian president Slobodan Milošević was put on trial. He died in custody in 2006 before a verdict was reached.
Cambodia (1997)	The tribunal has Cambodian and international judges and has sentenced three Khmer Rouge leaders to life imprisonment: ■ Nuon Chea, Khmer Rouge chief political ideologist ■ Kaing Guek Eav, head of the S21 mass killing centre ■ Khieu Samphan, the former head of state. The Court has also fulfilled an educational role by enabling Cambodians, especially those born after the genocide, to understand what happened during the 1970s.
Rwanda (1997)	The tribunal sentenced 61 individuals for complicity in the genocide. These included the former prime minister Jean Kambanda, who was sentenced to life imprisonment for genocide. The tribunal also established the legal precedent that rape can be used as a way of perpetrating genocide.
Sierra Leone (2002)	In 2012, Liberian president Charles Taylor was sentenced to 50 years' imprisonment for his role in fomenting the violence in Sierra Leone. Taylor is the first head of state to be convicted by an international tribunal. The tribunal has also imprisoned 15 others, including Augustine Gbao, a leading commander of Sierra Leone's Revolutionary United Front, who was sentenced to 25 years in prison.

Criticisms of United Nations tribunals

International tribunals have been accused of double standards and of implementing victors' justice:

- The NATO bombing of civilian targets in Serbia in 1999 has not been investigated by the tribunal.
- In the aftermath of the Rwandan genocide the Tutsi Rwandan Patriotic Front also massacred Hutus, but the Rwandan Tribunal ignored this.
- The Sierra Leone Tribunal has been funded by Western money, reinforcing a negative stereotype that African states cannot provide justice themselves.
- The establishment of UN tribunals has been inconsistent, undermining the UN's claim to be establishing new principles of impartial international justice. Saddam Hussein, for example, was tried by an Iraqi court established under the authority of the American occupation.

Knowledge check 22

What have been the main achievements of the United Nations tribunals?

The International Criminal Court

In 1998 the Rome Statute mandated the establishment of the International Criminal Court, and in 2002 it opened in The Hague. By 2017, 124 states had ratified the Rome Statute, which means that they accept the jurisdiction of the ICC.

International Criminal Court successes

- The existence of the ICC means that the principle of international justice is now permanently represented in international dialogue.
- Unlike the ICJ, the ICC has a chief prosecutor (Fatou Bensouda 2012–) who can initiate prosecutions on the authority of the Court.
- In 2016 Laurent Gbagbo, former head of state of Côte d'Ivoire, appeared before the ICC charged with crimes against humanity in the bloody aftermath of the country's disputed presidential election in 2010.
- By 2017 the ICC had convicted three Congolese war criminals (Thomas Lubanga Dyilo, Germain Katanga and Jean-Pierre Bemba).

Criticisms of the International Criminal Court

The effectiveness of the International Criminal Court is undermined by the fact that its liberal attempts to establish a universal standard of human rights protection often conflict with the realist self-interest of sovereign states:

- Three of the permanent members of the UN Security Council (China, Russia and the USA) refuse to accept the ICC's jurisdiction over their internal sovereign affairs. This dramatically undermines the authority of the Court.
- Influential emerging powers such as India and Turkey also do not recognise the ICC's authority, meaning that 70 per cent of the world's population is outside the jurisdiction of the Court.
- The ICC lacks coercive power. If states refuse to co-operate with its investigations, it cannot enforce compliance. ICC investigations into Sudanese president Omar al-Bashir and Kenyan president Uhuru Kenyatta have been dropped because of lack of co-operation.
- The ICC has been accused of having a neo-colonial Western bias against Africa. By 2017 the Court had indicted and convicted only Africans, leading to South Africa threatening to abandon the Court.
- The global influence of leaders such as Narendra Modi (India), Recep Tayyip Erdoğan (Turkey), Donald Trump (the United States) and Vladimir Putin (Russia) provides an increasingly nationalist alternative to the liberal cosmopolitan values of the Court.

Key issues in dealing with human rights

Impact on state sovereignty

According to liberalism, states achieve the most when they co-operate with each other. Liberals, therefore, regard institutions that enforce human rights and international law as a vital tool in creating a more stable world order based upon collective respect for international justice.

International Criminal Court (ICC) An intergovernmental organisation established by the Rome Statute (1998). It hears cases against individuals accused of war crimes, genocide and crimes against humanity.

Exam tip

It is important to use specific examples when you are answering exam questions on how effectively international law is enforced. This will provide your response with greater conviction.

Knowledge check 23

What are the main restraints on the effectiveness of the International Criminal Court?

Realists, however, respond that nation states are motivated by self-centred principles of what it is in their best interests to do. States, therefore, put immediate gain before that of the common good, meaning that in an anarchic world order, in which rules are unenforceable, sovereign self-interest generally triumphs over international law. Realists also claim that, according to Westphalian principles of state sovereignty, no other jurisdiction can legally intervene within the borders of a state.

Table 11 examines why it is so difficult to enforce an international standard of human rights.

Knowledge check 24

How do realist theory and liberal theory relate to the enforcement of a global standard of human rights?

Table 11 Why is it so difficult to enforce an international standard of human rights?

State sovereignty	All states possess sovereign authority in their internal affairs. This means that states often refuse to co-operate with institutions that seek to enforce international law. Human rights-based law is thus an example of soft law.
Inequality before the law	For international law to work, all states would need to be equally accountable for their actions. This is not the case since powerful states — like Russia, China and the United States — have acted in defiance of international human rights-based law without fear of the consequences.
Cultural relativity	In spite of the United Nations Declaration of Human Rights, there is no one universally accepted standard of human rights. Western powers focus on the rights of the individual; Muslim countries derive human rights from the Qur'an; Asian and Russian interpretations of human rights emphasise the good of the community over the well-being of the individual.
The three generations of human rights	Articles 3–21 of the Universal Declaration of Human Rights represent civil and political rights (first generation). There is dispute over whether Articles 22–27, which list social and economic rights (second generation), are of equal authority. Solidarity rights (third generation), such as gender, ethnic and gay rights, are even more controversial.

The rise of humanitarian intervention in the 1990s

Humanitarian intervention increased in the 1990s for a number of reasons:

- Since the Cold War was over, the UN Security Council was no longer divided between the United States and the Soviet Union, making action easier.
- Advances in broadcasting technology made human rights abuses more difficult to conceal.
- The establishment of UN safe havens to protect the Kurds in Iraq in 1991 challenged Westphalian principles of state sovereignty.
- The human suffering and potential for regional instability caused by inaction was shown by failures to intervene soon enough in Rwanda and Bosnia.
- UN secretary-generals Boutros Boutros Ghali and Kofi Annan put their moral weight behind humanitarian intervention.
- Influential leaders such as Bill Clinton (Clinton Doctrine, 1999) and Tony Blair (Chicago Speech, 1999) also made the moral and practical case for humanitarian intervention.

Exam tip

When examining the difficulties in enforcing a global standard of human rights, link to the section Theories of global politics (p.6), which highlights the ongoing importance of realism in global relations.

The United Nations Responsibility to Protect (2005) and the conflict with state sovereignty

In 2005 a United Nations World Summit endorsed the UN Responsibility to Protect. This established the principle that a state's sovereignty is 'conditional' upon it protecting its citizens' human rights. According to Responsibility to Protect, state sovereignty thus entails both rights *and* responsibilities. States are, therefore, expected to provide 'responsible sovereignty'. In this way Responsibility to Protect developed the liberal principle that there is an obligation to 'save strangers', based upon our shared humanity. This, of course, sets it at odds with the traditional realist interpretation of state sovereignty, which is that there is no legitimate authority above the nation state that can legally intervene within its borders.

Knowledge check 25

What are the main justifications for humanitarian intervention?

Why have some humanitarian interventions been more successful than others?

In order to be successful, a humanitarian intervention should have:

- sufficient military force
- a commitment to subsequent nation-building
- international/regional support
- realistic objectives

Table 12 illustrates the importance of these factors.

Table 12 A comparison of successful and unsuccessful humanitarian interventions

Unsuccessful interventions	Successful interventions
<ul><li>Somalia (1992–93)</li><li>Bosnia (UN intervention 1991–95)</li><li>Rwanda (1994)</li><li>Afghanistan (2001)</li><li>Iraq (2003)</li><li>Darfur (2007)</li><li>Libya (2011)</li></ul>	<ul><li>Bosnia (NATO intervention 1995)</li><li>Kosovo (1999)</li><li>East Timor (1999)</li><li>Sierra Leone (2000)</li><li>Côte d'Ivoire (2011)</li></ul>
These interventions failed to achieve their objectives because their aims were unrealistic (Somalia, Iraq, Afghanistan), they were too late (Rwanda, Darfur), they lacked legitimacy (Iraq) or there was insufficient commitment to military force or nation-building (Bosnia, Libya). Often these factors overlapped, leading to failure.	These interventions were more successful because sufficient military force was deployed (Bosnia, Kosovo) and there was a strong commitment to nation-building (Bosnia, Kosovo, East Timor). The objectives were realistic (Bosnia, Kosovo, Sierra Leone, Côte d'Ivoire, East Timor) and there was strong regional or international support for intervention (Bosnia, Kosovo, Sierra Leone, Côte d'Ivoire, East Timor). In most cases all of these criteria were fulfilled, so encouraging success.

Reasons for selective interventionism

For a humanitarian intervention to take place, world leaders need to be convinced of at least some of the following:

- that there are sufficient moral grounds to intervene
- that there is international or regional support for intervention
- that lack of action could threaten their interests
- that military force can resolve the conflict
- that intervention will not provoke a wider conflict

Table 13 looks at the reasons for specific interventions and non-interventions.

Table 13 Justification for interventions and non-interventions

Interventions	Non-interventions
Somalia: President George H.W. Bush believed an American intervention could 'end the starvation'.	Rwanda: None of the great powers had vital strategic interests in the region; the French government had strong connections with the Hutus; the United States had been scarred by loss of life in Somalia.
Bosnia: Following the Srebrenica massacre there was a strong moral case for NATO to intervene.	Darfur: There has been a lack of media coverage of atrocities; the UN Security Council has not agreed it is a 'genocide'; unwillingness to challenge Sudan's sovereignty.
Kosovo: Tony Blair argued that there was a moral case for NATO to intervene; inaction could lead to further war in the Balkans.	Zimbabwe: Zimbabwe is a sovereign state; Western intervention would be vetoed by Russia and China; Western intervention would be condemned as retro-colonialism.
East Timor: Australian-led UN-mandated intervention had a strong chance of success and would remove the threat of a refugee crisis.	Syria: Western powers have been unwilling to intervene against President Assad for fear of provoking wider conflict with Russia; US government is unprepared to commit to 'regime change' following bloodshed in Iraq.
Sierra Leone: Limited British intervention could end the fighting.	Tibet: The Chinese government has been accused of human rights abuses in Tibet. However, China is a powerful nuclear state and permanent member of the UN Security Council and so it would be impossible to intervene in its domestic affairs.
Afghanistan: The United States believed it was in its strategic interests to intervene following 9/11.	
Iraq: The Anglo-American intervention was primarily aimed at removing Saddam Hussein as a threat to regional and global stability.	
Libya: Colonel Gaddafi's threat to show 'no mercy' to the rebel town of Benghazi provoked a NATO response.	
Mali: The African Union supported French intervention to stop destabilising terrorist infiltration of Mali.	

Examples of alleged Western double standards and hypocrisy

Critics of humanitarian intervention argue that the selective nature of intervention indicates Western hypocrisy. A number of humanitarian crises have thus been ignored because it is not in the interests of the West to intervene. This is either because an ally of the West is involved (Gaza, Yemen) or because there are no vital interests involved (Rwanda, Darfur, Sri Lanka).

- Rwanda: in 1994, Western powers failed to intervene to stop the genocide.
- Gaza: from July to August 2014, the UN estimates 2,100 Palestinians were killed in the Gaza Strip during Israel's Operation Protective Edge; of these, 1,462 were civilians, including 495 children.
- Darfur: the UN estimates 300,000 have died since 2003 in Darfur as Sudan's government has tried to defeat its separatist movement.
- Sri Lanka: in 2009, UN reports suggest that 20,000 civilians may have been killed when government forces over-ran the Tamil Tigers' last redoubt in northeast Sri Lanka.

- Yemen: a Saudi-led alliance has killed thousands of civilians in air strikes against Houthi rebel forces.
- Syria: by 2017 the UN estimates that 400,000 may have died in this conflict. Western powers have been unwilling to intervene in case they provoke a wider conflict.

Summary

When you have completed this topic you should have a thorough knowledge of the following information and issues:

- Why the Universal Declaration of Human Rights was published.
- Why the International Court of Justice was established.
- The successes and failures of the International Court of Justice.
- Why the International Court of Justice is not more successful.
- Why the European Court of Human Rights was established.
- The effectiveness of the European Court of Human Rights.
- Why United Nations tribunals have been established.
- The effectiveness of United Nations tribunals.
- Why the International Criminal Court was established.
- The differences between the International Court of Justice and the International Criminal Court.
- The effectiveness of the International Criminal Court.
- The significance of the tension between human rights and state sovereignty.
- The significance of the UN Responsibility to Protect.
- The arguments for and against humanitarian intervention.
- Why some humanitarian interventions are more successful than others.
- Why humanitarian intervention is selective.

In addition, you should have gathered appropriate information to help you answer the following wide-ranging questions:

1 Examine how effective international courts are in upholding human rights.
2 Evaluate the extent to which human rights have become better protected since the end of the Cold War.
3 Examine why is it difficult to enforce a universal standard of human rights.
4 Evaluate to what extent the case for humanitarian intervention is convincing.

■ Global governance: Environmental

The role and significance of the United Nations Framework Convention on Climate Change

The **United Nations Framework Convention on Climate Change** was agreed to by 181 nation states at the Rio de Janeiro Earth Summit in 1992. The UNFCCC accepted the principle that climate change was being accelerated by human activity and that the global community needed to reduce its output of carbon, which was contributing to the so-called greenhouse effect. However, although the UNFCCC established a common agreement that action needed to be taken, it failed to achieve a consensus between the developed and the developing worlds about how the cost and burden of reducing reliance on fossil fuels should be balanced. On the principle of 'common but differentiated responsibilities', the UNFCCC anticipated that developed countries

United Nations Framework Convention on Climate Change (UNFCCC) Adopted at the Earth Summit in Rio de Janeiro in 1992. It recognises the importance of 'stabilizing greenhouse gas emissions' and so established the context in which all subsequent UN climate change conferences have taken place.

would take the lead in limiting emissions. This, though, proved highly controversial, especially in the United States, and so the UNFCCC's target of stabilising greenhouse gas emissions at 1990 levels by 2000 proved a dead letter. As would so often be the case in climate change negotiations, an inability to agree on fair burden-sharing thus undermined the case for action.

The role and significance of the Intergovernmental Panel on Climate Change

The **Intergovernmental Panel on Climate Change** was established under the auspices of the United Nations in 1988 to provide the most scientifically up-to-date assessment of the causes and likely effects of climate change on the planet. Its focus on achieving consensus between the world's most eminent climate change scientists and strict governmental neutrality has given it particular authority, so that its reports are treated with great respect. In 2007 its most dramatic and influential report stated that 'warming of the climate system is unequivocal' and that 'most of the observed increase in global average temperatures since the mid-20th century is very likely due to the observed increase in anthropogenic greenhouse gas concentrations'.

Competing views about how to tackle environmental issues

Since the 1970s there has been a growing appreciation of the need to ensure **sustainable development** for the good of the planet. This is because, as the reality of human-influenced climate change has become more widely accepted, so the need to find a global solution to the problem has become more pressing.

Environmentalism, however, also throws up sharp divisions between shallow and deep approaches to sustainable development.

Shallow-green ecology

Shallow ecology represents the reformist/mainstream approach to the problem of climate change. Its philosophical basis is in the work of Aldo Leopold, and its contemporary exponents include Anthony Weston. Shallow ecologists recognise that the actions of humans are influencing climate change and believe it is important that the global community takes action to reduce carbon emissions before it is too late. Shallow ecology, as its name implies, seeks to do this within existing free-market/capitalist economic structures and without diminishing economic growth or material well-being.

Shallow ecology is therefore optimistic, since it endeavours to resolve the problem of climate change through market forces and technological innovation.

Governments can also provide incentives to make green choices:
■ Since 2010 public hire bikes have been introduced into London and elsewhere, including Manchester, Oxford and Glasgow, in order to cut down on car use.

Intergovernmental Panel on Climate Change An intergovernmental body that provides the United Nations with objective scientific evidence about the origins, progress and impact of climate change.

Sustainability and **sustainable development** A type of development that meets the needs of the present without sacrificing the environmental well-being of future generations.

- A number of cities, including London, Stockholm and Milan, have introduced congestion charges to discourage traffic in city centres in order to improve air quality.
- There are a number of government incentives to install solar panels. In 2014, for example, the Domestic Renewal Heat Incentive was introduced in the UK to encourage householders to switch to renewable domestic heating systems.
- In the UK electric cars that cost less than £40,000 are exempt from road tax.
- Since 2015 all supermarkets in the UK have charged at least 5p for plastic bag use.
- The European Union requires member states to adopt energy-consumption labelling for most domestic appliances, so providing consumers with the information — and an incentive — to make green choices.

Green capitalism also provides consumer incentives to make environmentally friendly consumer decisions:

- As a result of their high performance and cheapness to run, electric cars are becoming increasingly fashionable. The popularity of the Tesla S and the Nissan Leaf electric vehicles are thus changing consumer habits by creating positive incentives to 'go green'. As consumers require more green automobile choices then, by the law of supply and demand, more car manufacturers will invest in this technology, demonstrating how capitalism can provide the initiative in addressing the problem of climate change.
- As domestic consumers and businesses seek to heat and light their homes more cost-effectively, this will create the incentive for architects to design buildings that are both attractive and low-cost to run. One Angel Square in Manchester was rated (2017) as the most energy-efficient building in the UK. Its iconic look and energy proficiency thus provide the incentive for other such building projects in the future.

Deep-green ecology

Deep ecology represents a much more radical approach to the environment. According to deep ecology, mainstream attempts to protect the environment are inherently flawed because they are motivated by the selfish desire to protect the material interests of humans at the least cost to themselves.

Deep ecology draws no distinction between the various types of life on Earth and instead works from the premise that we should protect the planet out of love and reverence for *all* the life that it provides for. Deep ecology therefore provides an idealistic justification for environmentalism, rather than the much more pragmatic attitude of shallow ecology which is motivated by the fear that inaction could spell disaster for humanity.

Arne Næss (1912–2009) coined the term 'deep ecology' to contrast it with shallow ecology which, he argued, is purely utilitarian and anthropocentric (human-centred). Rachel Carson (1907–64) further developed the principle that we must limit our global human footprint, and E.F. Schumacher (1911–77) questioned to what extent materialism and economic growth really were inevitable and desirable. Then in 1979 James Lovelock (1919–) popularised deep ecology in his 'Gaia' thesis, in which he argued that the Earth is a living being (Gaia) and that as such human beings have a duty to protect that which sustains them, out of love rather than self-interest.

Exam tip

Climate change provides a classic example of a collective dilemma, which liberals believe can be resolved only through organs of global governance. Realism, with its focus on state egoism, offers much less direction on communal problems such as this.

Deep ecologists thus demand a paradigm shift in how we interpret the environment. Rather than making the future of humanity the central proposition, they adopt an 'eco-centric' approach, whereby our impact, as a species, on the planet is as limited as possible. This is not for our own advantage, but because we have no right to unbalance the harmony of the biosphere by our greed. According to Satish Kumar (1936–), we thus need to educate ourselves to be 'eco-literate' so that at school we learn how to distinguish 'the oak, the ash and the elm'.

As a result of such a principled and uncompromising stance, deep ecology provides a much more radical approach to the environment, viewing shallow ecological strategies as piecemeal and ineffective because they are so self-serving. Capitalism, because it is based upon greed and exploitation, cannot therefore provide a way forward. Instead, a total re-think of our relationship with each other and with the planet is required so that we deal with the 'disease' itself rather than just its symptoms.

- Human beings should consume only that which they need to satisfy their essential needs.
- We must accept limitations on and restrictions of our lifestyles in order to rebalance the biosphere in favour of diversity.
- Governments should no longer prioritise economic growth. The Green Party in the UK is, for example, committed to allowing 'zero or negative growth'.

Sustainable development and the tragedy of the commons

Sustainable development represents development that fulfils our needs today without so damaging the environment that the well-being and survival of future generations are jeopardised. In 2015, the importance of sustainability was globally recognised when the United Nations initiated the UN Sustainable Development Goals (2015–30).

Although the prominence of sustainable development has increased in recent years, it has proved more difficult to achieve progress. This is because of what has been termed the **tragedy of the commons** thesis. Developed by the ecologist Garrett Hardin (1915–2003) in 1968, the concept of the tragedy of the commons begins with the historical example of the way in which the over-grazing of the common land by selfish individuals meant that it became useless for everybody. This greedy attitude is being replicated today but on a global scale, as nation states, transnational corporations and individual consumers put the gratification of their immediate wants before the sustainability of the **global commons**. The way, therefore, in which self-interest has been allowed to take priority over collective needs makes it much more difficult to make the necessary progress to combat climate change. As Garrett Hardin put it, 'Freedom in a commons brings ruin to all.'

Knowledge check 27

In what ways does the 'tragedy of the commons' help us to understand why it has been difficult to resolve the problem of climate change?

Knowledge check 26

Explain why there is so much tension between shallow and deep ecology approaches to the environment.

Tragedy of the commons
A term developed by Garrett Hardin in 1968. It refers to the way in which individual users put their own immediate interests before those of the wider community, so exhausting the common resources of all.

Global commons
Natural resources that are not owned by any nation state. The oceans, Antarctica, the atmosphere and outer space are all examples of the global commons, over which no individual state can claim jurisdiction.

Strengths and weaknesses of international climate change agreements

Table 14 Summary of the strengths and weaknesses of the Rio, Kyoto, Copenhagen and Paris climate change conferences

Treaty	Strengths	Weaknesses
Rio de Janeiro Earth Summit (1992)	■ Established the United Nations Framework Convention on Climate Change (UNFCCC), which recognised the importance of reducing carbon emissions in order to protect the environment. ■ 172 governments participated in the Earth Summit and 181 endorsed the principles of the UNFCCC. ■ A 'watershed' conference, in that for the first time close to a global consensus was achieved that the global community needed to address the problem of climate change. ■ The UNFCCC also required signatories to attend regular climate change conferences in order to evaluate progress.	■ The UNFCCC's emphasis on the importance of the developed world shouldering most of the burden of reducing carbon emissions proved so unpopular in the United States that it failed to engage with the UNFCCC and so did not provide necessary global leadership. ■ No specific or binding targets were agreed for reducing carbon emissions. ■ Since no monitoring procedures were authorised by the UNFCCC, nation states could not be held accountable for lack of progress.
Kyoto (1997)	■ The Kyoto Protocol set *binding* targets for 38 developed states and the European Union to a 5.2 per cent reduction on their carbon emissions compared to 1990 levels by 2012. ■ In 2005 the Kyoto Protocol came into force, when a sufficient number of states agreed to ratify it. ■ Kyoto also introduced carbon trading known as 'cap and trade', which provides governments with great flexibility in achieving their carbon reduction targets. If a government fails to reach its carbon reduction target, it can purchase 'credits' from those that have exceeded their targets. This therefore creates a financial incentive to surpass others' carbon reductions.	■ The targets that the Protocol set were widely controversial. The United States refused to ratify the Protocol because its target of a 7 per cent reduction of greenhouse gases by 2012 was seen by President George W. Bush as unfairly discriminatory. ■ The Protocol also failed to require the developing world to cut its carbon emissions, even though China's and India's rapid industrialisation was making them major polluters. ■ The necessary global consensus to resolve this 'collective dilemma' was thus not achieved; even worse, the divisions between the developing and developed worlds were publicly exposed.
Copenhagen (2009)	■ The unprecedented 110 heads of government who attended Copenhagen 'recognised' that global temperature increase should not be allowed to rise beyond 2 degrees above pre-industrial levels. ■ Agreement was reached that the developed world would annually invest, by 2020, $100 billion to encourage green technology in the developing world.	■ It proved impossible to achieve a consensus over how carbon reduction should be fairly shared between the developed and developing worlds. ■ As a result of this, no new binding targets were agreed.
Paris (2015)	■ At Paris a near global consensus was agreed that temperature increase in the twenty-first century must be limited to 2 degrees and, if possible, to 1.5 degrees. ■ Both the developed and developing worlds agreed to submit their own carbon reduction targets, known as Intended Nationally Determined Contributions (INDCs), enabling an agreement to be reached. The criteria for target-setting are that it should be 'ambitious' and exceed previous targets. ■ The INDCs will be regularly monitored in order to review progress.	■ Critics of the INDCs argue that even if they are fully adhered to, global temperatures will still dangerously increase by 2.7 degrees this century. ■ Although signatories to Paris are legally bound to provide their carbon reduction targets, and to have these monitored, the targets they set are not binding.

Obstacles to international co-operation and agreement

Sovereignty

A key reason why it has been so difficult to make more substantial progress on reducing carbon emissions is that states resent limitations being put on their sovereignty. This unwillingness by states to adopt externally imposed targets and legally enforceable targets thus explains why the United States was not prepared to adopt the Kyoto Protocol (1997) and why the Copenhagen Conference (2009) ended without mandatory cuts in emissions being agreed.

Realist 'state egoism', by which nation states prioritise their own immediate well-being, has thus made the resolution of a long-term collective dilemma such as climate change particularly difficult to resolve. Even the Paris Treaty (2015), which is generally seen as having been a success, was agreed *only* when states were allowed to negotiate their own Intended Nationally Determined Contributions (INDCs), without compliance being enforced by any supranational body. When in June 2017 President Trump withdrew the United States from its Paris Treaty INDC obligation to reduce carbon emissions by 26–28 per cent by 2025, he did so according to the 'national interest', declaring: 'I was elected to represent the citizens of Pittsburgh, not Paris. I promised I would exit or re-negotiate any deal which fails to serve America's interests.'

Developed versus developing world division and disagreement over responsibility and measurement

Differences between the developing and developed worlds have also undermined attempts to establish more ambitious and legally enforceable carbon reduction targets.

- The developed world has been polluting the planet with carbon since the Industrial Revolution in the eighteenth century, and so the developing world has argued that the developed world should bear a greater burden of the cost of limiting carbon emissions.
- Transnational corporations (TNCs) based in the developed world have often outsourced production to the developing world. Consequently, carbon emissions have increased in the Global South without the developed world being held responsible.
- It has been difficult achieving agreement on how pollution should be measured. The developed world has favoured measuring total output, which would make China the world's biggest polluter and focus attention on its responsibility for significantly cutting emissions. The developing world, with its burgeoning population, has preferred a 'per capita' measurement, which would make the United States a significantly greater polluter than China. Table 15, opposite, based on 2011 statistics, demonstrates how both China and the United States could claim the other is the bigger polluter and hence should bear greater responsibility for reducing its emissions.

> **Knowledge check 28**
>
> What have been the main strengths and weaknesses of climate change conferences?

> **Knowledge check 29**
>
> In what ways have the liberal intentions of the UNFCCC been undermined by realism's emphasis on the sovereign self-interest of the nation state?

Table 15 A comparison of Chinese and American carbon dioxide emissions, 2011

	Total carbon dioxide (million tonnes)	Per capita carbon dioxide emissions (tonnes of carbon dioxide per person)
China	8,716	6.5
United States	5,491	17.7

Since an equitable share of meeting the cost of carbon reduction is hard to agree, the Intended Nationally Determined Contributions (INDCs) committed to by countries in the developing and developed world are likely to remain controversial. President Trump's abandonment of the United States' Paris commitments is likely, therefore, to make the problem worse, since it may encourage other states to focus less on the collective good than on whether they feel they are being expected to contribute too much to resolve the problem.

This analysis may be too pessimistic, however. The uniqueness of the Trump presidency does not mean that his approach to international environmental co-operation will define American policy in years to come. Each climate change conference has also created greater global awareness of the problem, and regional organisations like the European Union, TNCs, consumers and subnational governments are all playing an increasingly significant role in addressing the problem. For example, the governors of the states of New York, California and Washington have all stated that that they will continue to comply with the requirements of the Paris Agreement: significantly, California, if it was a nation state, would have the sixth biggest economy in the world, so this commitment is important.

Knowledge check 30

How important do you think nation states are in resolving environmental problems?

The role and significance of civil society and non-state actors in addressing and resolving environmental issues

A key reason why climate change has achieved such global recognition is because international non-governmental organisations (NGOs) — such as Greenpeace, Friends of the Earth, Global Footprint Network and Citizens' Climate Lobby — have become a major part of the global debate. As a result of this, they have succeeded in raising awareness of the importance of climate change among the global public, as well as putting constant pressure on governments to seriously address the problem of climate change. World Earth Day (22 April each year) has thus been an initiative designed to focus global attention on the fragility of the planet, while green lobbyists constantly put pressure on governments and TNCs to go further in developing green agendas. Climate Change Network, for example, acts as an umbrella group for environmental NGOs and regularly lobbies meetings of the UNFCCC. As Chancellor of the Exchequer, George Osborne was put under such pressure by the green lobby that he even privately referred to them as the 'environmental Taliban'.

Summary

When you have completed this topic you should have a thorough knowledge of the following information and issues:

- The significance of the United Nations Framework Convention on Climate Change (UNFCCC).
- The reasons why the UN Intergovernmental Panel on Climate Change is so important.
- The justification for a shallow ecology approach to environmentalism.
- The philosophical basis of deep ecology, as well as the key thinkers associated with this movement.
- The contrasting ways in which shallow and deep ecology seek to tackle environmental problems.
- The meaning and significance of the tragedy of the commons thesis.
- What the following climate change summits did and did not achieve: Rio de Janeiro (1992), Kyoto (1997), Copenhagen (2009) and Paris (2015).
- The extent to which sovereignty and state egoism (realism) have made it more difficult to resolve the problem of climate change.
- Why it has been difficult to achieve a consensus between the developed and developing worlds on how best to approach the problem of climate change.

In addition, you should have gathered appropriate information to help you answer the following wide-ranging questions:

1 Examine the main reasons why greater efforts have not been made to address the problem of climate change.
2 Evaluate the extent to which differences between the developed and developing worlds undermine efforts to solve the threat of climate change.
3 Examine why shallow and deep ecology offer such different approaches to the environment.
4 Evaluate the extent to which significant progress has been made to limit temperature increase during the twenty-first century.

■ Power and developments

Different types of power

The use and effectiveness of hard power (military and economic)

The term 'hard power' was coined by the political theorist Joseph Nye and means coercive power. When hard power is deployed, this means force is used to achieve a desired outcome. This can be done through the use of military power, economic pressure and diplomatic manoeuvring. Realists often emphasise the utility of hard power. This is because realists view nation states as egotistical. In the resulting anarchic world system, the most effective way of achieving your objectives is thus through hard power because that is the only effective way of deterring the aggressive impulses of other states and so resolving the 'security dilemma' in your favour.

The great exponent of realpolitik, Otto von Bismarck, once remarked that, 'A conquering army on the border will not be stopped by eloquence.' The American gangster Al Capone echoed this mind-set when he said, 'You can get much further with a kind word and a gun than you can with a kind word alone.'

Hard power refers to the military and economic influence that can be deployed to force or coerce another power to act according to your wishes.

There are many examples of the effective utilisation of hard power:

- In the 1970s, Henry Kissinger brilliantly deployed his diplomatic skills to achieve détente (loosening of tension) with the Soviet Union. This was done by opening diplomatic relations with China. By so isolating the Soviet Union, this pressured it into reaching a nuclear settlement with the United States in the Strategic Arms Limitation Treaty (1972)
- The European Union utilises its huge economic influence when it negotiates trade deals on the World Trade Organization for all its members.
- The European Union also used its economic power when it imposed sanctions on Russia following its annexation of Crimea and on Belarus in order to encourage political reform.
- In 1991 military power was successfully deployed to remove Iraqi forces from Kuwait, and then military air power was successfully used to maintain safe havens within Iraq.
- In 1999 NATO used military power to stop Serbian ethnic cleansing in Kosovo.
- In 2011 NATO air power led to regime change in Libya.
- Russia deployed military hard power when it annexed Crimea in 2014.
- In 2017, President Trump used military hard power when 59 American tomahawk cruise missiles were launched against Syria following the regime's gas attack on civilians. This was to deter any further attack by President Assad since he would fully understand the consequences.

Critics of hard power point out that there are limits to what it can achieve. There are many examples of superior hard power not achieving the desired outcome. In Vietnam, Iraq and Afghanistan, superior military forces have been defeated by insurgents, and extensive sanctions on both Russia and Syria have not achieved a shift in the policies and priorities of those governments.

The use and effectiveness of soft power (diplomatic and cultural)

Joseph Nye contrasts hard power with **soft power**, which is the use of persuasion to achieve your objectives. This is done through the attractions of your culture and through political and social systems that encourage others to emulate you. Liberals often focus on soft power because it emphasises the potential for global co-operation based upon shared principles and interests.

Given the massive expansion of the internet and the spread of globalisation, the opportunity for advancing cultural and political values has never been greater, and so liberals maintain that soft power provides a cheaper, less chancy and more effective means to achieve one's objectives:

- One of the reasons for the collapse of the Soviet Union was that its communist ideology could not compete with the attractions of capitalist materialism. As the American satirist P.J. O'Rourke put it, communism collapsed because 'nobody wants to wear Bulgarian shoes'.
- According to former Foreign Secretary David Miliband, the global influence of the European Union primarily derives from it being a 'model power'. This is why other regional organisations like the Association of Southeast Asian Nations and the African Union have emulated it.

> **Knowledge check 31**
>
> Explain how hard power can be utilised in global politics.

> **Soft power** The utilisation of the attractions of a power's cultural appeal to persuade others to act according to its wishes.

- During the Vietnam War, US Defense Secretary Robert McNamara remarked that, as well as a military conflict, the war was a battle for 'hearts and minds'. Today, in the war against terror, pressure groups like the Quilliam Foundation emphasise that the only fully effective way to combat extremism is to achieve reconciliation and understanding between Muslim and non-Muslim communities.
- China is extending its international influence by opening Confucius Institutes globally. These are designed to promote an understanding of Chinese values, especially among young people.

Supporters of soft power thus argue that in order to achieve your objectives, you need to possess a more powerful narrative than that of your adversary. This is indispensable to success, especially in an age of instant communication. Russia, for example, has limited global outreach because it has such tiny soft power influence outside its near abroad.

Joseph Nye has also coined the term 'smart power' to show the way in which both soft and hard power can be used *together* to achieve one's objectives. The effective use of both superior American military power and its more attractive political ideology could thus be seen as an example of 'smart power' winning the Cold War.

Differing significance of states in global affairs and how and why state power is classified

Superpowers, great powers and emerging powers, including BRICS and MINT

Towards the end of the Second World War, the international relations theoretician W.T.R. Fox developed the term 'superpower' to refer to a nation state that could make its influence felt anywhere in the world at any time. During the Cold War, both the United States and the Soviet Union could claim superpower status because their military outreach and global alliances enabled them to assert their interests globally. Since the end of the Cold War, only the United States has been able to claim superpower status because it is unique in being able to exert diplomatic, military and economic influence anywhere in the world.

China, Russia, the United Kingdom and France are all examples of great powers. This is because they all possess significant military, economic and diplomatic influence. All of them have nuclear weapons and exercise the veto on the United Nations Security Council. They spend significant amounts on their militaries, are proactive in global affairs and have strong economies. However, none of them maintains anywhere close to the military and diplomatic outreach of the United States. China, for example, could be said to be a big dog in its backyard, while the United States is a big dog everywhere.

Emerging powers are often associated with the sorts of countries represented by the terms 'BRICS' and 'MINT'. Both of these mnemonics were thought up by the Goldman Sachs economist Jim O'Neill and refer to Brazil, Russia, India, China and South Africa (BRICS) and to Mexico, Indonesia, Nigeria and Turkey (MINT). These

Superpower In 1944 W.T.R. Fox defined a superpower as a great power with 'great mobility of power'. A superpower is thus a state that is able to make its military, economic, diplomatic and cultural appeal felt anywhere in the world.

Great power Great powers represent the most important states in global relations. They possess significant military influence and global interests and play a leading role in intergovernmental organisations.

Emerging power A power with an increasingly significant economic influence. As a result of this it is likely to play a growing role in international relations.

rising countries are seen as likely to achieve significantly greater global influence as a result of their developing economic influences, which have provided them with increasing self-confidence in international affairs. The European Union could, because of its increasing economic and diplomatic influence, also be defined as an emerging power.

Polarity

The implications of unipolarity/hegemony

Unipolarity refers to a global distribution of power in which there is just one dominant power. No other power can match its global influence and so that power can be referred to as the 'global hegemon'. When the Cold War ended in 1991, the United States achieved hegemonic status since its global influence dwarfed that of even its closest competitors.

The consequences of unipolarity for global stability are contested. According to the hegemonic stability theory, unipolarity can encourage international peace and security if the hegemon is generally well regarded as a 'benign' hegemon. This is because other states will 'bandwagon' behind the hegemon and, as the dominant power, the hegemon can be relied upon to maintain the status quo by the constructive utilisation of its global influence.

In the Ancient World, Rome's unrivalled political and military influence, together with the appeal of Roman culture, established a Pax Romana, which maintained peace and stability for over three centuries. In the nineteenth century, Great Britain's naval supremacy provided it with global dominance. In the 1990s, the United States' unparalleled economic, military and diplomatic outreach, together with the popularity of its culture, established the conditions for American hegemony. The political scientist Charles Krauthammer thus refers to the 1990s as the United States' 'unipolar moment'.

Critics of unipolarity argue that it does not maintain stability. This is because states are 'power maximisers' and so the hegemonic status of one power will always generate resentment among second-tier powers, which covet its influence. This situation is at its most dangerous if the superpower is perceived as weakening, since it can lead to the volatility of power transition. This creates the potential for conflict as the superpower seeks to retain its influence in response to increasingly powerful challenges from its rivals. According to some historians, the First World War was provoked because Germany felt that it could now bid to challenge Britain's global influence. Today, one of the greatest threats to global stability comes from Chinese and Russian attempts to test the limits of the United States' power.

The radical theorist Noam Chomsky has also focused on the implications of what has been termed 'malign hegemony', arguing that unipolarity destabilises global relations because a hegemon can act in defiance of international law and conventions. American foreign policy during the administration of George W. Bush (2001–09), when the United States acted in defiance of institutions of global governance such as the United Nations, provides an example of this.

Knowledge check 32

Using examples, explain the main differences between great powers and superpowers.

Unipolarity refers to the dominance of one single power in international relations. So great is the economic, military and diplomatic influence of this power over others that it achieves hegemonic status.

Knowledge check 33

Why is hegemonic stability theory controversial?

Exam tip

Be prepared to contextualise your writing on unipolarity, bipolarity and multipolarity within the realist–liberal debate.

The implications of bipolarity

Realists such as Kenneth Waltz argue that **bipolarity** provides the greatest potential for global stability. This is because the aggressive impulses of each of two superpowers will be restricted by the other. Since each superpower will maintain global alliances, the rivalry between the two states will, rather than creating conflict, thus achieve a global balance of power or equilibrium.

The Cold War rivalry of the Soviet Union and the United States (c.1945–c.1991) is seen by realists as the classic example of bipolar equilibrium. Since neither side was capable of destroying the other, this created the conditions for a stable equilibrium.

Critics of bipolarity argue that this is a simplistic interpretation of the Cold War. There was a constant jockeying for influence between the two sides, which resulted in numerous proxy wars in Korea, Vietnam, South America and Africa. Bipolarity also encourages distrust and suspicion, which is why the Cuban Missile Crisis (October 1962) came so close to provoking nuclear disaster. The Ancient Greek historian Thucydides highlighted the inherent dangers in bipolarity when he argued that it was the constant rivalry between Athens and Sparta that made the Peloponnesian War inevitable.

Therefore, according to liberals, bipolarity only *superficially* provides peace. Global relations, far from being stable, are instead in constant flux as each superpower seeks to undermine the other, so creating the constant potential for conflict.

The implications of multipolarity

When global relations are multipolar, this means that four or more powers are competing for global influence (three powers competing is known as tripolarity). The period between the First and Second World Wars (1918–39) could be seen as a period of **multipolarity** since power was shared between a number of existing and emerging great powers, including Great Britain, Germany, France, the Soviet Union, Japan and Italy.

The consequences of multipolarity also divide realists and liberals. Realists dislike multipolarity because they associate it with anarchy. Without a global leader (unipolarity) or the rivalry of two powers (bipolarity), they argue it is much more difficult to achieve a balance of power. Evenly matched states will therefore be continually shifting alliances and seeking to expand their military, economic and diplomatic influence at the expense of their rivals. This creates the ever-present potential for conflict. When politics is multipolar there is therefore minimal trust and constant flux since there are no restraints on the aggressive tendencies of states.

Liberals are more optimistic about multipolarity. They argue that states are just as likely to work together as to compete and so in a multipolar world there are greater opportunities for co-operation between states, since the potential for global harmony is not undermined by bipolar rivalry or hegemonic excess. For a multipolar world to be peaceful, however, nation states need to be prepared to accept the authority of institutions of global governance, such as the United Nations.

Bipolarity refers to a global distribution of power in which two competing superpowers are relatively equally matched in terms of global influence. Their rivalry will thus dominate international relations.

Knowledge check 34

Why do realists and liberals disagree about the consequences of bipolarity for global stability?

Multipolarity denotes an international distribution of power in which numerous powers compete for global influence.

Exam tip

Be prepared to deploy precisely learned historical examples when writing about the consequences of the various types of polarity for global stability.

How has the balance of world power changed since 2000?

Since 2000 the balance of global power has developed in a number of ways. At the beginning of the century, American hegemony seemed unrivalled. Indeed, a number of leading members of the George W. Bush administration were committed to what was called 'The Project for the New American Century', which would extend US hegemony far into the new century.

However, although no other power can yet challenge American dominance, many political commentators believe that the balance of global power is gradually moving away from hegemonic stability and towards multipolarity:

- By 2020, the Chinese economy is expected to be greater than that of the United States.
- China is already militarily challenging American influence in the South China Sea.
- The economy of the European Union is greater than that of the United States, allowing the EU to negotiate — on equal terms with the United States — the Trans-Atlantic Trade and Investment Partnership.
- Russia is beginning to assert its influence in Europe, going to war with Georgia in 2008 and annexing Crimea from Ukraine in 2014. Russia is also playing an increasingly assertive role in the Middle East, especially in the Syrian Civil War.
- As a result of bloody interventions in Afghanistan and Iraq, the Obama administration (2009–17) often stepped back from its global responsibilities, failing to provide effective leadership during the Arab Uprisings.
- The rise of cyber technology now provides any state and some non-state actors with the potential to wield enormous power, potentially 'flattening out the world' in terms of the distribution of power.

Different systems of government

The characteristics and consequences for global order of democratic, semi-democratic, autocratic, failed and rogue states

According to the democratic peace thesis, **democratic states** are unlikely to go to war with each other. This is because democratically accountable leaders know that risking conflict with other democracies will not increase their prestige. Francis Fukuyama thus predicted in his end of history thesis that, as liberal democracy spread in the aftermath of the fall of communism, so war between nation states would become less likely. The spread of democracy would thus extend 'zones of peace' at the expense of 'zones of conflict'.

On the other hand, **semi-democratic states** and **autocratic or non-democratic states** can seek to increase their popularity in an aggressive fashion in order to increase national prestige and so provide (false) legitimacy for the government. In 1982, for example, Argentina's military junta invaded the Falkland Islands in order to win easy political popularity. In 1990, Saddam Hussein did the same when Iraq invaded Kuwait.

Knowledge check 35

Why is there so much disagreement about the consequences of multipolarity?

Democratic state A democratic state is one in which the government is freely elected by the public through universal suffrage and in which the government is held accountable for its actions through regular and fair elections.

Semi-democratic state combines elements of democracy with authoritarianism. For example, although there may be regular elections, some parties may be banned and the media may be censored.

Autocratic or non-democratic state places unlimited power in the hands of an unelected leadership that is not accountable to its citizens. An autocratic state will therefore not possess democratic legitimacy.

Rogue and failed states have a particularly negative impact on global stability. **Rogue states** act purely out of self-interest and ignore international law if it suits their interests to do so. This then creates uncertainty and instability. North Korea has thus been termed a rogue state because its leadership ignores the Treaty on the Non-Proliferation of Nuclear Weapons (1968) and continually acts in an aggressive fashion, in defiance of international condemnation.

Failed states encourage the spread of chaos and anarchy. This is because the government of a failed state can no longer ensure its citizens' security and so criminal gangs and terrorist organisations can thrive among the lawlessness. Yemen, Somalia, Afghanistan, Iraq and Syria have all been termed failed or failing states because their governments have been unable to stop large parts of their countries becoming ungovernable. As a result of this, criminal and terrorist organisations have been able to use these states as bases for national, regional and even global operations.

The development and spread of liberal economics, the rule of law and democracy

Since the end of the Cold War in 1991, liberals have argued that the spread of democracy, the rule of law and free trade has encouraged peace and co-operation. The more democratic a state, therefore, the more likely it is to obey international standards of behaviour and the less likely it is to provoke conflict by engaging in nationalist, religious or ethnic rivalries with its neighbours.

According to Immanuel Kant (1724–1804), this is because:

- democracies possess internal checks and balances that reduce the risk of just one person deciding on war
- democracies will be more likely to co-operate with each other in liberal institutions of global governance
- the lucrative connections that free trade establishes between states mean that war will be economically self-defeating for all states involved — Thomas Friedman has referred to this as the 'Dell Theory of Conflict Prevention'.

The ways and extent to which changes in global power address and resolve contemporary global issues involving conflict, poverty, human rights and the environment

The changing balance of global power may make it more difficult to address and resolve these contemporary global issues:

- Growing challenges to the United States' global hegemony are likely to result in the potential for conflict as emerging powers, such as China and Russia, test the limits of American power. Since the United States, unlike Great Britain after the Second World War, is not prepared to relinquish its global influence, this will result in the potential instability of power transition.
- The rise of Russia and China has provided an alternative model to democracies, so challenging the optimistic post-Cold War belief that the global spread of democracy was inevitable.

Rogue state An authoritarian state that acts in defiance of globally accepted standards of international law. By doing this it encourages both regional and global instability.

Failed state A state where the government has disintegrated, so creating a power vacuum. The resulting anarchy and violence will threaten its neighbours and, potentially, the wider global community.

- Authoritarian governments such as China and Russia focus less on individual human rights than on the communal good of society.
- The failure of the Arab Spring to encourage the spread of democracy in the Arab world has demonstrated the enduring influence of authoritarian governments.
- As a result of the global economic crisis, nation states have increasingly put their own national interests ahead of those of the global community. This provides one explanation for the election of President Trump and the rise of populism in Europe. This may make it more difficult to resolve collective dilemmas such as climate change.

Summary

When you have completed this topic you should have a thorough knowledge of the following information and issues:

- The significance of hard power in international relations.
- The significance of soft power in international relations.
- The difference between superpowers and great powers.
- The definition of emerging powers and their significance to the international balance of power.
- The meaning of unipolarity and its consequences for global order.
- The meaning of bipolarity and its consequences for global order.
- The meaning of multipolarity and its consequences for global order.
- The extent to which the global balance of power has changed since 2000.
- The significance for global stability of democratic and authoritarian states.

- The way in which failed states and rogue states negatively impact on global stability.
- The way in which the spread of democracy and free trade encourages global stability.
- The significance for global stability of contemporary developments in the balance of power.

In addition, you should have gathered appropriate information to help you answer the following wide-ranging questions:

1 Evaluate the extent to which it is important for nation states to exert soft power in order to achieve their objectives.
2 Explain why realists regard unipolarity and bipolarity as more likely than multipolarity to ensure global stability.
3 Evaluate the extent to which contemporary global relations are now multipolar.
4 Explain what you think are the main threats and challenges to contemporary global stability.

■ Regionalism and the European Union

The growth of regionalism and its different forms

Regionalism is the process by which nation states that inhabit the same region decide their interests are best served by becoming more closely integrated. In the process, nation states agree to pool sovereignty to a greater or lesser extent in order to achieve better desired outcomes for themselves.

Regionalism The process by which greater collective action and closer relations are established between nation states within the same geographical location.

Economic regionalism

Economic regionalism is the process by which nation states within the same geographical location eliminate or significantly reduce customs barriers (tariffs) between them. As a result of this a free-trade area is created, so encouraging greater regional trade and investment. A further advantage of economic regionalism is that nation states which are represented by powerful regional organisations can wield greater influence when negotiating trade deals.

Political regionalism

Political regionalism refers to the way in which nation states in a similar area that share related political and cultural beliefs decide they can wield greater diplomatic influence by co-operating. By establishing regional organisations, such as the Arab League or the African Union, they can therefore be represented with a more unified and powerful voice in international negotiations.

Security regionalism

Nation states embark upon security regionalism in order to enhance their safety. This can be done in two ways. By working more closely together, nation states in a similar geographical location increase the trust between them. By engaging with each other in 'crisis management' and providing peace-keepers, they also further reduce the risk of conflict. The Organization for Security and Co-operation in Europe (OSCE) is a good example of this. Regional organisations can also increase a region's security by deterring hostile intervention from other powers. One of the reasons for the establishment of the Association of Southeast Asian Nations (ASEAN) was to protect its members from China and Japan.

Debates about, the reasons for and the significance of regionalism

The relationship between regionalism and globalisation

The growth of regionalism and globalisation are closely connected for a number of economic and security reasons:

- Nation states decide that, by combining in regional organisations, they will be more able to take advantage of the economic opportunities offered by globalisation. This is because the increased power of regional organisations means that they will be more able to negotiate successful outcomes in international trade deals than if they act alone. For example, the European Union negotiates as one body on the World Trade Organization, providing it with huge comparative influence.
- If regions are more closely integrated, this can also mean they can protect themselves more efficiently from foreign competition by erecting regional barriers and encouraging regional subsidies. The European Union thus protects its agricultural sector through tariffs and by subsidies represented by the Common Agricultural Policy.
- Globalisation also creates significant security challenges for nation states since crime, terrorism, online radicalisation, and people- and drug-trafficking reach across borders. By working together, regions are better able to protect themselves.

ASEAN is committed to establishing closer co-operation between its members in order to more efficiently confront security challenges. Europol has established a more co-ordinated European response to the security challenges its members face.

Prospects for political regionalism and regional governance

The prospects for the further development of regionalism are disputed. Realists point out that the nation state remains the primary actor in global politics. The Brexit referendum result, together with the rise of Donald Trump and his 'America First' criticisms of the North American Free Trade Agreement (NAFTA), provide stark warnings against liberal assumptions that the nation state is being hollowed out by globalisation.

Further developments of regionalism have also advanced the prospects for increased regional governance, however:

- In spite of Brexit, the European Union continues to enlarge. Turkey, Macedonia, Albania, Montenegro and Serbia are all candidates for membership (2017).
- Within the EU there is a strong movement for full unity associated with federalists like Guy Verhofstadt, leader of the Alliance of Liberals and Democrats for Europe group.
- The African Union is planning a single market and single currency by 2023.
- Integral to ASEAN's 2020 vision is the encouragement of a common regional identity among its member states: 'outward-looking, living in peace, stability and prosperity, bonded together in partnership in dynamic development and in a community of caring societies'.

The impact on state sovereignty

When nation states join regional organisations, they agree to work more closely together. In economic regional organisations, the member states establish freer trade and employment relations between them, and in political and security regional organisations they seek to achieve greater interdependence, co-operation and cohesion. This challenges a nation state's claims to absolute sovereignty. The European Union, as the most advanced form of regionalism, has most impacted on member states' sovereignty. Regional organisations are still established by treaties, however, and so member states may reclaim their sovereignty. For instance, President Trump has threatened to withdraw from NAFTA. Since the EU has no absolute claim to sovereignty over the states that comprise it, Article 50 of the Lisbon Treaty allows member states to leave.

Knowledge check 36

Explain the ways in which regionalism is a response to globalisation.

Development of regional organisations, excluding the EU

North American Free Trade Agreement

NAFTA was established in 1994 between the United States, Mexico and Canada. Its aim is to create a free-trade area by eliminating tariffs (protectionism) between these countries. It is thus an example of economic regionalism and, unlike the European

Union, it does not seek greater political integration. Its sole purpose is to encourage greater trade within the North American continent. For example, trade between the United States and Mexico increased by 506 per cent between 1993 and 2012, and between the United States and non-NAFTA countries by 279 per cent in the same period. In 2011 American trade with its NAFTA partners was greater than its trade with Japan, South Korea, India, China and Brazil combined.

African Union

The Organization of African Union (OAU) was created in 1963 in response to the ending of colonial rule. Its purpose was to promote co-operation between the newly independent states on social and security issues. In 2002, the OAU was replaced with the more ambitious African Union (AU), which is closely modelled on the European Union and seeks to encourage pan-African peace, security and economic co-operation among its 54 members. Its institutions include a parliament and a Peace and Security Council. The heads of all its governments meet every year at an assembly and a commission implements AU policies.

Although the African Union aims to become more unified, it is still primarily an intergovernmental organisation (IGO). It does, however, aspire to emulate the integration achieved by the EU, so it has both economic and political functions and aspirations. African Union peace-keepers have worked with the United Nations in Darfur and Somalia, and the African Union's New Partnership for Africa's Development (NEPAD) provides a unified bargaining tool for African states when negotiating for Western aid and investment. There are also plans to establish a central bank, a human rights court and, by 2023, an African Economic Community based upon a single currency.

Arab League

The Arab League was established in 1945. It is an example of political and security regionalism since it seeks to encourage peace and stability within the region and because it represents the views of Arab states in international dialogue. The Arab League's most important body is the council, to which each member of the League sends delegates twice a year. A general secretariat is in charge of administration and the League is represented by a secretary-general.

Since each member of the League possesses the veto and the League has no supranational authority, its effectiveness is limited. Although its members share cultural similarities, the religious and power struggles within the Arab world have undermined its influence. It was unable, therefore, to offer a unified Arab response during either the 1991 or 2003 Gulf Wars.

During recent crises, however, it has managed a more coherent response. In 2011, Libya was suspended from membership in response to Colonel Gaddafi's suppression of the opposition, and the Arab League supported the UN's decision to authorise air-strikes. Syria has also been suspended from the League and the League has endorsed Saudi Arabia's intervention in Yemen against Houthi rebels. In 2015 the principle of a Joint Arab Force was established to counter extremism and terrorism in the region.

Knowledge check 37

Explain, using examples, the different reasons why regional organisations are established.

Association of Southeast Asian Nations

The Association of Southeast Asian Nations (ASEAN) was set up in 1967 to encourage regional growth and provide a counter-weight to the regional superpowers China and Japan. It models itself on the European Union and is committed to the creation of an 'ASEAN community', based on closer economic, political and security co-operation. It has negotiated free-trade agreements between its members, introduced visa-free travel and allowed limited free movement of professionals. Members of ASEAN also share intelligence on terrorist threats and pledge not to acquire weapons of mass destruction. Its greatest political success has been putting pressure on Myanmar to introduce democratic reforms. It has been less successful in establishing a co-ordinated response to Chinese territorial claims in the South China Sea.

Factors that have fostered European integration and the major developments through which this has occurred

Formation, role, objectives and development of the European Union

In contrast to other regional organisations, the **European Union** owes its existence to a moral imperative. **Federalism** has thus always been a driving force in the European Union as the nation states of Europe more closely integrate with each other.

Key figures in its establishment, such as Robert Schuman and Jean Monnet, saw **European integration** as a necessary way of avoiding further European bloodshed following the First and Second World Wars. These wars had been caused by rampant nationalism, and so the process of European integration was designed to create the economic links *and* the political links between countries that would make another European war impossible. In addition to this, European economic integration would encourage greater prosperity, and a more united Europe would have greater geo-strategic influence, especially in regard to the perceived threat from the Soviet Union. As a result of globalisation, the European Union has also deployed its influence to negotiate better economic deals for its members with IGOs such as the World Trade Organization.

The European Union has gradually evolved:

- The Schuman Declaration (1950) provided the basis for the European Coal and Steel Community (1951). By pooling these vital military materials, war between members would be made impossible.
- The success of the European Coal and Steel Community led to the Treaty of Rome (1957), which established the European Economic Community based upon the principle of ever-closer union between the peoples of Europe.
- In 1993, as a result of the Maastricht Treaty, the European Community became the European Union, based upon a common European citizenship.

Exam tip

Remember that every regional body was set up for its own specific reasons. Just because the European Union has achieved the most economic and political union does not mean that it is the most successful.

European Union (EU) The most advanced example of regionalism. In 1957 the Treaty of Rome established the European Economic Community (EEC). In 1993, as a result of the Treaty of Maastricht, it became the European Union.

Federalism European federalism can be interpreted in two ways. Euro-sceptics usually deploy the term to indicate 'ever-closer union' in a European super-state. In contrast, the European Union defines federalism as *balancing* power between central and regional bodies.

European integration The process by which an 'ever-closer union' is created between members of the European Union.

Content Guidance

The key institutions of the European Union

Table 16 Summary of the functions of the main institutions of the European Union

The Commission	This is the executive arm or 'government' of the European Union, which recommends legislation. The 28 commissioners are appointed and represent the interests of Europe rather than of their own state. The President of the Commission is nominated by the leaders of the European member states and confirmed by the Parliament. In 2014, Jean-Claude Juncker became President of the Commission. (Supranational)
The Council of Ministers	The Council of Ministers is attended by each member state's minister as appropriate. Thus, if the Council is discussing environmental issues, each state's environment minister will attend. The Council is the main legislating body of the European Union and decides whether or not to accept proposals. Members can put forward their national interests on this body. Some decisions still need to be unanimous (so protecting national sovereignty), although decisions are increasingly being made by Qualified Majority Voting (QMV). (Intergovernmental/supranational)
The European Council	The European Council comprises the heads of all the EU governments. It meets four times a year and since 2014 its President has been Donald Tusk. It establishes and drives forward the overall direction and purpose of the European Union. (Intergovernmental)
The Parliament	The Parliament is the EU's only directly elected body. Members of the European Parliament (MEPs) sit according to political rather than national groupings. The Parliament shares some legislative powers with the Council of Ministers, known as 'co-decision'. Its main powers, however, lie in scrutinising legislation through committees. As the power of last resort, it can dismiss the Commission and reject the budget. (Supranational)
The European Court of Justice	Since European law is binding on member states, the European Court of Justice adjudicates in cases where there is dispute between national and European law. It ensures that European law is upheld equally throughout the EU. (Supranational)
The European Central Bank	The European Central Bank controls monetary policy, setting interest rates for members of the eurozone. Since 2011, Mario Draghi has been head of the Central Bank. (Supranational)

The process of enlargement

- By expanding, the European Union entrenches democracy within states. According to the liberal democratic peace thesis, democracies are unlikely to go to war with each other.
- The establishment of free trade and the free movement of people further encourages peace, prosperity and stability. This is the principle that 'If goods do not cross borders, armies will.'
- A larger European Union also provides European nation states with greater geo-strategic influence in IGOs or when negotiating directly with powerful states like Russia, China or the United States.

Table 17 The development and expansion of the European Economic Community and European Union

1957 Treaty of Rome establishes the European Economic Community	The founding members of the EEC are France, West Germany, Italy, Belgium, the Netherlands and Luxembourg.
1973–95	In 1973 the first enlargement of the EEC occurred, when the UK, Ireland and Denmark join. As other Western European states join, membership increases to 15 by 2004.
2004	The European Union dramatically expands to 25 members. Eight of these new members are former East European Communist states. As a result of this, the European Union now covers most of the continent.
2007	Bulgaria and Romania join the European Union.
2013	Croatia joins the European Union. Membership rises to 28.

Key treaties and agreements

The dramatic expansion of the European Union raises the problem that it might become so economically and culturally heterogeneous that it could expand into irrelevance. Therefore, it is important to balance widening–deepening so that the EU *both* expands *and* becomes more closely integrated.

Since its establishment, a series of treaties have encouraged the process of 'ever-closer union' between the members of the EEC/EU. These treaties have been designed to ensure that although the EEC/EU has widened, it has also been possible to deepen the relationship between its members. 'Ever-closer union' does not though necessarily mean greater centralisation or a European super-state. The principle of European 'federalism' is that power should be shared between central and more local government, and this has been recognised through subsidiarity. The following treaties have been particularly important in shaping the European Union:

- The Single European Act (1986): This established the principle of a common European market and increased Qualified Majority Voting (QMV) on the Council of Ministers.
- Maastricht Treaty (1992): This re-established the European Community as a union with a common citizenship, ensuring that EU citizens can work anywhere in the EU and can vote in local and European elections wherever they live. Maastricht's Social Chapter also guaranteed European workers greater rights. It set three ambitious targets for a much more closely integrated European Union: a common currency by 2002, a common foreign and security policy, and greater co-operation in justice and domestic affairs. The principle that decisions should be made at a European Union level only if they cannot better be made at a local, regional or national level (subsidiarity) was also enshrined in the Maastricht Treaty.
- Amsterdam Treaty (1997): This further advanced the principle of European integration. The Schengen Agreement was incorporated into European law, ensuring passport-free travel between all EU states except the UK and Ireland. Further QMV was deployed on the Council of Ministers and greater democratisation was encouraged by increasing opportunities for 'co-decision' between the Parliament and the Council of Ministers.
- Lisbon Treaty (2007): As a result of the dramatic enlargement of the EU in 2004 and 2007, the Lisbon Treaty was designed to ensure that the EU did not become so diverse that it widened into just a loose confederation. It came into force in 2009. Therefore, the EU was provided with a legal identity to allow it to negotiate treaties and establish its own diplomatic service. The positions of EU President of the Council and High Commissioner for Foreign Affairs were also introduced, and QMV was further extended on the Council of Ministers.

Economic and monetary union

Since the Single European Act (1986), all European treaties have advanced the economic unity of the European Union. The establishment of a eurozone in 2002, of which 19 of the 28 members of the EU are now members (2017), has further advanced economic unity. The European sovereign debt crisis, which was provoked by over-spending by Greece, has also led to greater unified control of public spending (Fiscal Compact 2012) in order to achieve greater convergence between the economies of the eurozone.

Widening–deepening refers to the way in which the European Union has widened in terms of membership, but also deepened in terms of integration. There can be an uneasy relationship between 'widening and deepening', because a larger and more diverse EU may be more difficult to integrate.

Exam tip

Be careful how you use the term 'federalism'. Although Euro-sceptics in the UK have often used it as another way of referring to a European 'super-state', the precise meaning of federalism is a sharing of power between central and more local forms of government.

Knowledge check 38

Explain the tension between 'broadening and deepening' within the European Union.

Since all new members of the European Union must join the euro, and now that the UK has voted to leave the European Union, there will be growing pressure for all existing members of the European Union to adopt the common currency. If full economic and monetary union is thus achieved, the pressure for full political union may become unstoppable.

Debates about supranational versus intergovernmental approaches

The European Union has always been a balancing act between intergovernmentalism and supranationalism:

- An **intergovernmental** approach to the EU regards it as serving the interests of its member states. The member states thus pool sovereignty when it is in their interests to do so.
- A more **supranational** approach to the European Union regards 'ever-closer union' as a goal in itself and seeks to achieve complete European unity, whereby nation states are merged within fully unified supranational economic and political structures.

The competing claims of intergovernmentalism and supanationalism have often led to conflict over what the ultimate goal of the European Union should be. Intergovernmentalists emphasise the principle of subsidiarity as a way of protecting national sovereignty, so ensuring that the EU does not become more centralised. According to supranationalists, the EU must ultimately become a nation state like the United States, in order to better protect all its citizens and to wield maximum global influence. Guy Verhofstadt's book *Europe's Last Chance: Why the European States Must Form a More Perfect Union* (2017) provides a modern summary of the case for a more supranational European Union.

Significance of the EU as an international body/global actor

At the Treaty of Maastricht (1992), the European Union committed itself to achieving a common security and foreign policy. This is essential if the European Union is to become a significant **global actor**. As a result of the Lisbon Treaty (2007) the positions of European President and High Commissioner for Foreign Affairs were also created, in order to enable the EU to negotiate more effectively with other powers.

In what ways can the European Union exert global influence?

Economic

The EU is the world's largest economic and trading bloc. This provides it with substantial economic hard power:

- The EU can utilise this power by imposing economic sanctions on states (Russia, Syria, Zimbabwe).
- The attractions of its market can also be used by the EU to advance its interests and ideals. The Cotonou Agreement, for example, requires developing countries to safeguard human rights if they are to gain favourable access to European markets.

Intergovernmentalism The process by which decisions are reached between nation states, rather than being imposed on them from above.

Supranationalism refers to the process by which decisions are taken by institutions above the nation state. These institutions possess the authority to enforce obedience from the nation state.

Knowledge check 39

Provide examples of supranational and intergovernmental institutions within the European Union. Why does the European Union have both?

Global actor A nation state or non-state actor, such as a regional or non-governmental organisation, which plays a significant role in international relations.

- By working together on IGOs, such as the World Trade Organization, the EU can deploy its combined economic strength to maximum advantage.
- By combining its economic power, the EU can negotiate favourable deals with powerful nation states. In 2016, Turkey agreed to tighten up the flow of Syrian refugees into Europe in return for access to the Schengen zone and 're-energised' talks on Turkish membership of the EU.

Political/structural

As a result of the Lisbon Treaty, the EU now has its own legal identity and full-term Council President (Donald Tusk 2014–) and High Commissioner for Foreign Affairs (Federica Mogherini 2014–). This provides the EU with significant structural power in institutions of global governance so that it can help shape their development:

- The EU is represented on IGOs such as the World Trade Organization, G7 and G20.
- At the Paris Climate Change Conference in 2015, the EU negotiated as one body on behalf of all its members.

Military

- Since 2002, the European Union has had a rapid reaction force. It has been deployed in the EU's 'near abroad' (Macedonia and Bosnia) and further afield (Central African Republic and Democratic Republic of Congo).
- The EU has pooled its naval and intelligence forces, combatting pirates off the Horn of Africa (Operation Atalanta). It has also established a joint naval command to combat people-smugglers acting out of Libya.

Soft power

- According to former Foreign Secretary David Miliband, an effective way in which the EU can assert global influence is as a 'model power' that other states and regional organisations seek to emulate.
- ASEAN and the African Union have in some ways modelled themselves on the European Union, and the EU has provided global leadership by the extent to which it has committed itself to dramatically decreasing its carbon emissions.

Constraints and obstacles affecting the EU's political, economic, structural and military influence in global politics

Why has the EU not been able to exert more global influence?

- Foreign policy is still subject to the national veto. This means that the EU can only represent a unified foreign policy if all member states agree. This is difficult to achieve as member states often possess different geo-strategic objectives. It has, for example, been difficult to achieve a common EU approach to the Syrian Civil War or the Russian annexation of Crimea.
- Most EU states are also members of NATO and so they often rely upon NATO to represent their security/strategic interests.

- The EU can deploy a rapid reaction force, but it does not have its own army. This significantly undermines its potential to be taken seriously in international relations.
- According to the right-wing political writer Robert Kagan, European states have become so 'risk averse' that they are not prepared to provide a military lead in international crises. In 2017, only five European member states spent more than 2 per cent of their budgets on defence. The United States spent 3.3 per cent of its GDP on defence in 2017.

The ways and extent to which regionalism addresses and resolves contemporary global issues involving conflict, poverty, human rights and the environment

Regional organisations are playing an increasingly significant role in addressing conflict, poverty, human rights and the environment. For example:

- Since 2008 the African Union and the United Nations have together deployed a peace-keeping mission (UNAMID) in Darfur.
- The Organization for Security and Co-operation in Europe (OSCE) is monitoring the Minsk Accords (2015) in order to reduce the fighting in eastern Ukraine.
- The European Union is utilising its huge economic influence to encourage greater respect for human rights, as well as encouraging overseas development. The Cotonou Agreement, for example, requires African, Caribbean and Pacific countries (ACP) to enhance their record on human rights and democracy in order to achieve favourable terms of trade and increased aid from the European Union.
- The European Union adopted the Kyoto Protocol and dramatically exceeded its carbon-reduction target. It is thus providing a global lead in combatting climate change by setting itself the ambitious target of reducing its greenhouse gas emissions by 2030 by 40 per cent, compared with 1990 levels.

Opponents of regionalism, however, point out that it can have a negative impact. The Eurasian Customs Union has been criticised as a means by which Russia is seeking to re-establish influence in its near abroad with potentially destabilising consequences. The European Union has also used its enormous economic weight to try to negotiate favourable trade deals on the World Trade Organization, to the detriment of the developing world. This has been a major reason why the Doha Round of trade talks, aimed at making trade fairer for the developing world, has not been more successful.

Knowledge check 40

Why is the European Union often seen as being a unique example of regionalism?

Summary

When you have completed this topic you should have a thorough knowledge of the following information and issues:

- The various reasons why nation states join together in regional organisations.
- In what ways regionalism and globalisation are connected.
- The origins, successes and failures of NAFTA, ASEAN, the African Union and the Arab League.
- Why the EEC/EU was established.
- The extent to which the EU is both widening and deepening.
- The way in which EU treaties and agreements (Single European Act, Maastricht, Amsterdam, Lisbon and the Fiscal Compact) have advanced European integration.
- The difference between intergovernmentalism and supranationalism, and why this is significant.
- The significance of subsidiarity.
- The ways in which the EU exerts global influence.
- The reasons why the EU's global influence has been limited.

In addition, you should have gathered appropriate information to help you answer the following wide-ranging questions:

1 Evaluate the extent to which the European Union is a unique example of regionalism.
2 Explain the various reasons why regional organisations have been established.
3 Evaluate the extent to which the European Union is a successful organisation.
4 Explain what the main obstacles are to greater integration within regions.

Questions & Answers

■ How to use this section

Once you have familiarised yourself with the structure of this paper and the significance of the assessment objectives (AOs) (see below), you should work hard on mastering the best way of answering the questions. Sections A, B and C each require a different approach and if you are going to maximise your potential it is really important that you understand *exactly* what the examiners require for each.

This section of the book includes the types of questions you will find in Sections A, B and C, with example answers. The strengths and weaknesses of each specimen answer are indicated in the commentaries by the icon ⓔ. Do not try to memorise these essays, but do discuss them with your teacher and other students. If you can have a clear idea in your mind of the template for a top-level response in each of the three sections, then you will be well on the way to achieving success on this paper.

The key features of Paper 3: Comparative Politics — Global Politics

- The written examination is a 2-hour paper.
- It is worth one-third of your total A-level mark.
- The paper is worth 84 marks in total.

Section A	One question from a choice of two 12 marks 15 minutes	AO1 Knowledge and understanding (6 marks) AO2 Analysis (6 marks)
Section B	One compulsory question 12 marks 15 minutes For this question, you must 'discuss any relevant core political ideas' in your response. You should thus utilise your knowledge of socialism, liberalism and/or conservatism.	AO1 Knowledge and understanding (6 marks) AO2 Analysis (6 marks)
Section C	Two essays from a choice of three 30 marks each 45 minutes each Total: 90 minutes	AO1 Knowledge and understanding (10 marks) AO2 Analysis (10 marks) AO3 Evaluation (10 marks)

Assessment objectives

There are three assessment objectives (AOs), with a specific number of marks awarded for each (see table above). It is therefore really important that you understand what each one requires and where each of them is needed. When you are writing your answers you thus need to be constantly reflecting on whether you are fulfilling the AOs. This is a sure way of being able to achieve a top grade.

- **AO1 Knowledge and understanding:** This AO requires you to show an awareness of the key political ideas, facts and processes. This includes an awareness of contemporary evidence.

- **AO2 Analysis:** This AO requires you to apply your knowledge to the key word(s) in the question or example by making connections, showing an awareness of relevant similarities or differences, and showing an understanding of the changing nature of political systems. Remember that Section B requires you to apply one or more core theories (socialism, liberalism, conservatism).

- **AO3 Evaluation:** This AO requires you to develop arguments, make judgements (especially about the strengths of arguments) and come to conclusions. It applies only to Section C.

■ Section A questions

- You need to answer one 12-mark question from a choice of two.
- You have only 15 minutes to answer this question. You should very quickly jot down the main points you will investigate and then focus on making sure that every point you raise directly answers the question. In brief pieces of writing such as this, narrative or vague responses will be quickly exposed!
- There are up to 6 marks available for AO1 and 6 marks for AO2.
- All questions in this section ask you to 'examine'.
- You will impress the examiner if you cover three or four points/paragraphs. Include contemporary evidence *and* relate it to the question asked. Remember, too, that precise detail will show real conviction and thus impress the examiner.

Power and developments

Question 1

Examine the effectiveness of bipolarity and multipolarity in encouraging global stability.

(12 marks)

Student answer

When global politics is bipolar, global relations are dominated by two superpowers. A multipolar distribution of global power means that influence is shared between four or more equally balanced powers. The consequences of bipolarity and multipolarity for global stability profoundly divide political theorists. Some, like Kenneth Waltz, a noted defensive realist, argue that bipolarity can encourage stability since it creates a balance and equilibrium that it is not in the interest of either side to break. Others are more sceptical about the implications of bipolarity and counter that a multipolar balance of power can encourage co-operation and interdependence between nation states.

e The student usefully shows clear understanding of what both terms mean. The reference to Kenneth Waltz indicates the sort of detailed knowledge that will gain high marks for AO1. The explanation of the implications of both terms shows, too, that the student is already bidding for AO2.

It has been suggested that a multipolar world is the most unstable possible, because there will be a constant jockeying for power among nation states. As some achieve greater power than others, through either arms build-ups or alliances, so the chance of conflict is always there. A bipolar world, on the other hand, provides some protection from this sort of inherent instability. This is because two pre-eminent powers will be so evenly matched that there is no incentive for them to risk conflict with each other. Since each side will be able to exert its influence globally, the balance that it is in their interests to achieve will also be enforceable globally.

(e) This paragraph is very strong. The explanation is very clear indeed and it is impressive how the student is able to explain some quite complicated ideas so sharply. Both AO1 and AO2 can be awarded highly here.

In August 1990, while the Soviet Union still existed, the eminent political philosopher John Mearsheimer wrote an essay entitled 'Why we will soon miss the Cold War'. He concluded it with the prophetic words: 'If the Cold War is truly behind us, therefore, the stability of the past forty-five years is not likely to be seen again in the coming decades.' This is a powerful argument, because during the Cold War neither the Soviet Union nor the United States saw it as being in their interests to gamble on war. This, therefore, preserved peace in Europe for 45 years, from 1945 to 1990. Indeed, bipolarity even created opportunities for limited collaboration, since neither side was able to eliminate the other. For example, during the period of détente, the Strategic Arms Limitation Treaty (SALT) was signed between the Soviet Union and the United States in 1972, and in 1975 the Helsinki Accords (generally seen as being the high point of détente) recognised the permanence of the post-war borders of Europe.

(e) The student's use of John Mearsheimer is highly effective, especially since evidence is then deployed to substantiate his optimistic interpretation of the Cold War. AO1 continues to be strong, while phrases such as 'This is a powerful argument, because...' provide an excellent way of accessing AO2.

Critics respond that bipolarity is inherently unstable and dangerous. It has been said that peace is not simply the absence of war, and this can be related to the Cold War. Far from establishing an equilibrium, mutual suspicion created the sort of tension that could have erupted into war. An example of this is the Cuban Missile Crisis in 1962, when the attempt by the Soviet Union to put nuclear missiles in Cuba led to President Kennedy's quarantine of the island, which could have provoked armed conflict. Similar tensions can also be seen during the first Reagan administration (1981–85) when his arms build-up created huge tensions with the Soviet Union. Multipolarity, though, provides opportunities for co-operation just as much as conflict, as well as possessing none of the inherent suspicions associated with bipolarity. Instead, it enables nation states to become more interdependent through organs of global governance such as the United Nations, World Trade Organization and International Monetary Fund. J.D. Bowen, a liberal theorist, uses the analogy of a 'college campus' to explain how such a multipolar distribution of power can be to the advantage of all who participate in it. The different assessments of bipolarity and multipolarity thus depend not only upon different interpretations of history but on conflicting explanations of what motivates the behaviour of human beings and nation states.

(e) The final paragraph provides a very clear critique of bipolarity, especially because precise detail is utilised to support these arguments. This is followed by a very sound explanation of why some critics see advantages in multipolarity.

This is clearly a Level 4 response. The student provides a large number of relevant and accurate examples (AO1) and it is notable how the implications of these are then drawn out (AO2). As a result of this, the writing is coherent and evaluative throughout. There are no purely narrative paragraphs and the concluding sentence sharply encapsulates the core reasons for the two interpretations.

ⓔ Level 4: 12/12 marks awarded

Global governance: Economic

Question 2

Examine the divisions that exist between neo-classical development theory and world systems theory.

(12 marks)

Student answer

In the twentieth century Friedrich Hayek and Milton Friedman developed neo-liberalism and, in the wake of the Thatcher and Reagan years and the collapse of Communism, it became the dominant economic creed, often referred to as the 'Washington Consensus' or 'economic globalisation'. Its supporters maintain that nation states achieve economic prosperity by opening themselves up for trade and investment by reducing tariffs, subsidies and corporation taxes. By doing this, global trade is dramatically increased and nation states across the world increase their wealth by having the opportunity to sell their goods on a global rather than simply a national or regional level. By creating a global marketplace, the potential for further enhancing prosperity is therefore virtually limitless because there are no limitations on where you can buy, sell or produce. The World Bank and International Monetary Fund have encouraged this neo-liberal economic model through free-market structural adjustment programmes, while the World Trade Organization is based on the principle that tariffs and subsidies should be reduced as much as possible in order to create the most level playing field possible for trade and investment.

ⓔ The student deploys some very well-selected detail here and explains the way in which neo-liberalism can be seen to encourage prosperity. This means that AO1 and AO2 are both equally impressive.

As a result of the globalisation of neo-liberalism, global trade has indeed dramatically increased. In 2005 it was worth $8 trillion and by 2013 it was worth $18.8 trillion. The growing convergence between the Global North and Global South has thus been attributed to neo-liberalism, as has the relative success of the Millennium Development Goals. This is because the developing world has been able to break out of subsistence economics into global trade, with all the possibilities and opportunities this offers. In short, neo-classical development theory roots itself in the belief that individuals drive forward prosperity by being free to achieve what they wish with as little state interference as possible.

e This paragraph, although quite brief, is highly focused and drives forward the argument for neo-liberalism. The evidence is well selected and the understanding is clear.

In contrast, world systems development theory is rooted in a socialist interpretation of the global economy. According to one of its main exponents, Immanuel Wallerstein, global free markets, far from creating prosperity for all, actually reinforce a neo-colonial world order in which core states in the Global North are able to continue exploiting peripheral states in the Global South. This is because, by encouraging them to open up their markets, they are able to swamp them with cheap manufactured products so that they never succeed in achieving a proto-industrial stage of development. In addition to this, the wide availability of cheap labour in the developing world is then exploited by transnational corporations, encouraging a race to the bottom in terms of workers' pay, rights and conditions, as developing states compete with each other to attract foreign investment. The Rana Plaza factory disaster in 2013 is a good example of this, as the building collapsed because investors were trying to maximise their profits by ignoring safety standards. Thus, far from encouraging convergence, global free markets have created greater inequality than ever before, as can be seen in the way in which the Gini Coefficient measure of inequality has dramatically increased across both the developed and developing worlds.

e Pleasingly, the student demonstrates an equally incisive understanding of world systems theory and appropriately supports it, ensuring that there is real balance to the writing.

There is thus a clear division between the emphasis that neo-liberals put upon free markets as a way of encouraging greater global wealth, and the more negative response of world systems theory that economic globalisation has created a more globally unequal society than ever before based upon the global exploitation of the working class. As we have recently seen, the way in which neo-classical development theory generates wealth has ensured its dominance. As economic globalisation continues to undermine job security and to exacerbate social tensions and economic inequality, however, world systems theory offers for many on the left a more attractive analysis of how the global economy is best managed.

e This final paragraph helpfully sums up the main points of difference between the two contrasting theories. Since the ideas covered have been quite complicated it is helpful to have such a clear and forthright analysis of what the student sees as being the key issues. The reference to contemporary attitudes provides the essay with a memorable end that demonstrates the student has a real 'feel' for the significance of the material.

The student deservedly achieves full marks because the response is clearly rooted in a sharp understanding of both concepts. All sentences focus on answering the question and the detail is well selected. This is a response that possesses real conviction.

ⓔ **Level 4: 12/12 marks awarded**

Global governance: Environmental

Question 3

Examine the criticisms that have been made of both the deep and the shallow ecology approaches to climate change. (12 marks)

> **Student answer**
>
> Deep and shallow ecological strategies are very controversial because they approach environmental problems so differently. Shallow ecology wants to 'tinker around the edges', while deep ecology wants much more to be done in order to resolve the problem of climate change.

ⓔ An examiner will be concerned about an introduction like this. It is clear that the student understands the difference between the two interpretations. Unfortunately, though, the paragraph is too short for the ideas to be effectively developed, while the use of language like 'tinkering around the edges' is worryingly vague and imprecise. This sort of colloquialism should have no place in a piece of academic writing and has already undermined the examiner's confidence in this response.

> The deep ecological approach to climate change is based in the ideas of people like Arne Næss and Rachel Carson, who see the world as a living being or 'Gaia'. It is therefore really important that human beings protect it because the world protects them. Deep ecology therefore offers really radical solutions to the problem of climate change. For example, the Green Party in the UK is in favour of zero economic growth, and deep ecology generally states that, if we are to survive as a species, we need to dramatically limit our obsession with consumerism and materialism.

ⓔ This is proving a very frustrating essay to mark. The student has clearly revised and wants to do well. But too often the ideas are only partially remembered and understood. For example, 'Gaia' is actually associated with James Lovelock, while a main criticism of deep ecology is that it is not 'human-centred', so the reference to 'if we are to survive as a species' entirely misses the point of deep ecology.

> Deep ecology has been criticised because the solutions it offers to the problem of the environment are so radical that no government would ever be likely to implement them. The 'idealism' of deep ecology thus means that what it offers is unlikely to occur in reality.

e This is a better paragraph, but it could be improved if it was more closely connected to the previous paragraph, since this would more firmly establish the relationship between AO1 and AO2.

> The criticisms of shallow ecology are that it is 'too little, too late'. Shallow ecologists believe that the existing free-market/capitalist structure of global society does not need to be dramatically changed. Instead, 'green capitalism' and climate change agreements such as the Paris Treaty (2015) will be sufficient to ensure that global temperature rise is not above 2 degrees in the twenty-first century. Deep ecologists dislike the fact that this strategy is motivated by human self-interest rather than genuine 'love' for the planet, while even non-deep ecologists have been critical of what they see as the complacency of this approach to a potentially apocalyptic problem.

e This is quite a good paragraph. AO1 and AO2 are better connected and, although there is not that much detail, there is greater clarity of understanding.

Although the student has some understanding of the subject, it is too often superficial and occasionally misunderstood. More precise detail and a willingness to deploy more accurate terminology would raise the level considerably. As it is, the response cannot get beyond Level 2.

e **Level 2: 5/12 marks awarded**

■ Section B questions

- You need to answer one compulsory 12-mark question.
- As in Section A, you have 15 minutes to answer this question, so it is vital that you are focused and direct and that you deploy precisely selected detail.
- There are up to 6 marks available for AO1 and 6 marks for AO2.
- All questions ask you to 'analyse'.
- The main difference from Section A is that you are required to focus on realism and liberalism and in your answer to apply one or more of the core political ideas that are covered in Component 1 (socialism, liberalism and conservatism).

The state and globalisation

Question 4

Analyse the differences that exist between liberals and realists in regard to the importance of the nation state in global politics.

In your answer you must discuss any relevant core political ideas. (12 marks)

> **Student answer**
>
> The role and significance of the nation state in international relations lie at the heart of the liberal–realist debate. For realists, the ways in which nation states react with each other is, and should continue to be, at the core of international relations. In response, liberals argue that global politics is much more polycentric and that the centrality of nation states in decision-making needs to be challenged by un-egotistical institutions of global governance.

ℯ This introduction is clear and precise and, although the student uses some quite difficult language, he/she does so in an accessible and relevant fashion.

> According to realists, global politics is defined by anarchism. The proto-conservative thinker Thomas Hobbes in *Leviathan* (1651) summed up this sort of leaderless confusion as a state of nature in which 'there is continual feare, and danger of violent death; and the life of man, solitary, poore, nasty, brutish, and short'. A modern conservative thinker, Michael Oakeshott, took this further, reinforcing Machiavelli's negative view of humanity as imperfect and unpredictable, so requiring the nation state to protect its citizens from predatory impulses. Realists agree that there is no 'night watchman' (John Mearsheimer) to ensure and restore order and that, as a result of this, nation states can only rely upon themselves for their own protection. Classical realism, by emphasising human beings' tendency towards avarice and violence, can be used to further justify a strong nation state as the surest way to protect its citizens from the acquisitiveness of other governments. Structural realism, too, recognises the essential primacy of the nation state, since it alone can provide

security in a world based upon the self-interested rivalry of states, all of which seek to advance their national interests while disregarding the best interests of others.

e There is a very great deal in this paragraph. The detail is strong so AO1 can be well rewarded, and the explanations are skilful, especially of classical and structural realism, so the student also achieves highly in AO2. The use of Hobbes and Oakeshott as conservative thinkers satisfies the requirement to utilise core theory from Component 1.

Realism therefore focuses on the sovereign equality of all states. According to Westphalian principles of state sovereignty, global stability is best ensured if states respect each other's territorial integrity and do not deploy moral pretexts in order to intervene within the affairs of another state. In order to further ensure peace, nation states should build up their defences in order to deter the potential aggression of others, on the principle that it is the weaknesses of states rather than their strengths that provoke war. In short, realism states that the establishment of a pragmatic balance of power between states creates the best chance for peace, rather than 'muddle-headed and idealistic' attempts to act according to liberal principles of universal humanity. This has certainly been the attitude of Donald Trump, who in 2017 asked Congress to increase US military spending by $54 billion.

e The implications of realism are sharply explained and the references to Westphalian principles and the balance of power are well justified. The contemporary reference to Donald Trump works well.

Liberals respond that nation states destroy peace, rather than guaranteeing it. The President of the EU Commission, Jean-Claude Juncker, has called borders 'the worst invention ever', and liberals argue that it is state egoism that has been the main cause of war, as nation states seek to advance their own interests rather than the collective good. This is why Woodrow Wilson was so committed to the establishment of the League of Nations at the end of the First World War; a war that had been provoked by unrestrained state egoism. The socialist focus of Marx and Engels on our common humanity further challenges the nation state and, as the problems that humanity faces become increasingly interrelated, liberals argue that collective solutions are required to collective dilemmas. This is true of problems such as rogue states, nuclear proliferation and climate change, which nation states acting purely out of egotistical self-interest cannot resolve themselves. Liberalism, therefore, views the nation state as just one decision-making body in an increasingly globalised world of mutual dependence, in which numerous non-state actors, such as intergovernmental and non-governmental organisations, need to co-operate in order to achieve mutually beneficial goals. So long as the egoism of nation states is the main driving force in international relations, the authority of liberal organisations of global governance such as the United Nations will be fatally undermined.

ⓔ This is an excellent paragraph. The liberal perspective is very clearly explained and the references to globalisation and collective dilemmas provide appropriate context. The reference to Marx and Engels is possibly surprising but it works, reinforcing the sense that the student understands the requirements of a Section B response.

> The differences between realists and liberals over the role of the nation state are thus profound. Realists view a strong nation state as the only barrier against conflict, while liberals see the rivalry of nation states as the main cause of war! Such a dichotomy of opinion cannot easily be bridged and suggests that the status and utility of nation states will continue to sharply divide political opinion, especially in the context of Brexit and the rise of nationalist leaders such as Donald Trump.

ⓔ The final paragraph provides a helpful analysis of why the differences between realism and liberalism over the nation state are so important, and ends with a fitting reference to contemporary events.

This response is a pleasure to read. The student grapples with some highly complicated ideas but succeeds in doing so in a clear and accessible fashion — possibly because the sentences are well focused and generally not too long. This answer shows how a student who really understands a topic, from both a theoretical and a practical level, can achieve very highly indeed.

ⓔ **Level 4: 12/12 marks awarded**

Global governance: Human rights

Question 5

Analyse the significance of the divisions regarding human rights that exist between liberals and realists.

In your answer you must discuss any relevant core political ideas.

(12 marks)

Student answer

Liberals emphasise the importance of encouraging a global community through free trade and through mutual understanding and interdependence based on institutions of global governance such as the United Nations. The establishment of such international harmony is closely connected with a global acceptance of a universal standard of human rights that all nation states will be bound to obey. The Charter of the United Nations (1945) and its Universal Declaration of Human Rights (1948) thus represent a liberal approach to world affairs, in which nation states accept the importance of acting according to moral standards that are equally applicable anywhere in the world. As the Universal Declaration of Human Rights powerfully states in its opening paragraph, it seeks to protect 'the inherent dignity' of all human beings and to ensure 'the equal and inalienable rights of all members of the human family'.

---

e This opening paragraph is impressive because it immediately contextualises the question within the core political idea of liberalism. This ensures that the examiner will be confident that the student is, *right from the start*, obeying the specific demands of the question. The quotation from the Universal Declaration of Human Rights adds to the conviction of this response.

As early as the seventeenth century John Locke developed the liberal theory of limited government whereby governments cannot impose arbitrary rule, so that as members of a state we are citizens rather than simply subjects. John Stuart Mill then took this concept further in the nineteenth century, arguing that governments should not seek to impose their own moral views on how we live our lives (so long as we do not harm others by our actions). In other words, our intrinsic human rights are protected by the limits put on government to mould us in ways that it would like. More recently, the conservative philosopher Robert Nozick has taken this theory even further with his libertarian view of 'self-ownership'.

---

e This paragraph cleverly enables the student to fulfil the AO2 requirement that core political ideas from Component 1 are covered. Three philosophers (two liberal and one conservative) are introduced and their ideas are effectively used to drive forward the quality of the answer. There is no need for any more in-depth analysis than this.

Although this liberal emphasis on the centrality of our human rights has been responsible for the establishment of a number of UN war crimes tribunals, as well as the International Criminal Court in 2002, the further development of global human rights has been undermined by the ongoing importance of a more realist approach to international relations. This is because realism focuses on the centrality of the state in determining the civil liberties of its citizens, as well as rejecting a universal standard of human rights that can be imposed upon a sovereign state by outside influences.

ⓔ Although a brief paragraph, this is helpful because it signposts three important factors that the student is right to focus on.

State sovereignty represents a particular challenge for a universal standard of human rights. This is because, according to Westphalian principles of state sovereignty, nation states possess supreme authority within their borders, meaning that no external body can exert legitimate authority within a sovereign state. This is well illustrated by the fact that Russia, China and the United States have not been prepared to accept the authority of the International Criminal Court in cases involving their own citizens, while prosecutions of two African leaders — Omar al-Bashir (Sudan) and Uhuru Kenyatta (Kenya) — have been dropped because neither state was prepared to co-operate with the ICC. Even the United Kingdom, which prides itself on being the world's oldest liberal democracy, can prioritise its sovereignty over a supranational interpretation of human rights, such as when the UK parliament refused to allow prisoners the vote even though this is required by the European Convention on Human Rights. A particularly dramatic example of the clash between the liberal intentions of the Universal Declaration of Human Rights and realist state sovereignty is illustrated by the way in which Saudi Arabian law imposes the death penalty for converting from Islam to another religion. This law conflicts with Article 17 of the Universal Declaration of Human Rights, which requires religious freedom, and has been globally condemned, but Saudi Arabia has made clear that it will not compromise with the international community.

ⓔ There is a great deal to reward in this paragraph. There are lots of well-selected examples deployed so the student achieves highly at AO1, and also clear analysis of why they are significant, so ensuring that AO2 can also be awarded highly. The paragraph has clear momentum, too, ensuring that the evidence builds up well in a persuasive fashion.

Saudi Arabia's refusal to accept the principle of religious freedom also demonstrates that there is no one universal standard of human rights. Realist critics of such liberal universalism point out that it is based very much upon eighteenth-century European Enlightenment ideals and that these cannot actually claim to be globally applicable. Islam, for example, provides a very different religious interpretation of human rights to the secularism inherent in the Universal Declaration of Human Rights. Asian values, which focus on the rights of the community over those of the individual, and so can be used to justify the death penalty throughout most of Asia, further undermine the liberal concept of a global standard of human rights. In Russia, too, the Orthodox Church maintains a highly conservative approach to homosexuality and individual freedom, focusing instead on the duties one has to the wider community or *mir*.

ⓔ Here the evidence about Saudi Arabia in the previous paragraph is neatly carried forward to explain the argument that cultural relativity defines the extent of the rights that we are allowed rather than a universal standard of human rights. The examples are again well selected, although possibly some specific examples could have been included, such as the highly controversial punishment of Raif Badawi in Saudi Arabia for acting in defiance of Saudi religious law.

The way, therefore, in which realists emphasise the primacy of the state in determining the nature and extent of our civil liberties demonstrates why liberal attempts to advance universally applicable and enforceable standards of human rights have not been more successful. Indeed, so long as realism remains such a dominant political ideology, it is difficult to see how institutions such as the International Criminal Court or the European Court of Human Rights will be able to achieve the ambitions of their founders.

ⓔ This is a good paragraph that focuses well on the question by addressing why the differences between realism and liberalism are so significant in regard to human rights enforcement.

This response comfortably achieves full marks. The student is well informed and writes in a highly evaluative fashion, so the requirements of both AO1 and AO2 are clearly fulfilled. The core political ideas are neatly deployed and the demands of the question are continually addressed.

ⓔ **Level 4: 12/12 marks awarded**

■ Section C questions

- You will answer two 30-mark questions from a choice of three.
- Spend 45 minutes (including planning) on each answer.
- There are up to 10 marks for each of AO1, AO2 and AO3.
- Remember that AO3 is examined only in Section C.
- All questions will ask you to 'evaluate'. You evaluate by making judgements about the strengths of certain ideas or arguments. It is important to do this throughout your answer.
- A useful approach is to write an introduction, then either to write a series of arguments and counter-arguments or to write a series of arguments with evaluation of each argument, followed by a conclusion.
- You need, therefore, to write a balanced response that considers both sides of an argument, before reaching a well-justified conclusion.

Power and developments

Question 6

Evaluate the extent to which hard power is the most important type of power in global politics.

You must consider this view and the alternative to this view in a balanced way.   (30 marks)

> **Student answer**
>
> According to realist political philosophers such as John Mearsheimer and Kenneth Waltz, hard power represents the unrivalled currency in international relations. This is because the centrality of the sovereign nation state means that global politics is anarchic, in that there is no supreme 'Leviathan' that can impose international order. Therefore, military, economic and diplomatic hard power is required to protect a nation state from potential aggression from any quarter. Liberals, in particular, question the extent to which hard power really is the most important type of power in an increasingly interconnected and globalised world of instantaneous communication, in which your culture has the power to repel or attract virtually anyone anywhere in the world.

e This is a nicely focused introduction. It is clear that the student understands the meaning of the key terms and his/her use of Mearsheimer and Waltz, together with the deployment of 'Leviathan' in an appropriate context, indicates that this will be a well-supported, highly focused and intellectually self-confident essay.

When Joseph Nye coined the terms 'hard' and 'soft power' in 1990, he saw hard power primarily as a way of compelling others to act according to your wishes. Hard power is, therefore, often manifested through military action. One could argue, for example, that the British recovery of the Falklands Islands from Argentinian occupation in 1982 was only achieved because the task force was despatched and Argentinian forces were subsequently defeated. Similarly, the Russian annexation of Crimea in 2014 was effectively achieved through the calculated use of military power in Russia's near abroad. Realists would argue, too, that fanatical organisations such as so-called Islamic State cannot be stopped through dialogue and that, therefore, they need to be crushed by military action. President Obama, for example, frequently deployed drone strikes against al-Qaeda, while the liberation of cities like Raqqa from Islamist control requires the deployment of considerable military force in order to be effective. President Theodore Roosevelt (1901–09) certainly understood the value of hard power when he commented 'speak softly but carry a big stick', and realists would point out that military power provides the surest way of both protecting yourself from aggression and putting pressure on other nation states to adopt policies favourable to you. According to John Mearsheimer, nation states achieve much more by acting like Godzilla rather than Bambi, and the way in which Israel has survived the hostility of its neighbours since 1948 could be seen as demonstrating the utility of hard power in ensuring survival in an anarchic world order. As the master of realpolitik, Otto von Bismarck, put it in 1867, 'A conquering army on the border will not be stopped by eloquence.'

e There is a lot of very well-selected information here (AO1), which the student appreciates how to deploy in an analytical fashion (AO2). The reference to Joseph Nye is nicely handled and the quotations are introduced in a really appropriate context.

Liberals, however, point out that reliance on military power to achieve security and influence can be self-defeating. This is because arms build-ups encourage arms races, so a nation state's actions may actually end up increasing the security dilemma by placing it in a destabilising arms race with other nation states. In addition to this, Israel's emphasis on military power as its main guarantee of security has not resolved the threats it faces that remain existential. In the same way, Russia's annexation of Crimea has achieved its *immediate* strategic objectives, but at the expense of its suspension from the G8 and a dramatic rise in tension between Russia and the EU and NATO.

e This is a very helpful paragraph since it shows the student beginning to also bid for AO3. This is because there is an appreciation that there is a debate about the extent to which hard power really is effective and that there may be alternative ways for nation states to achieve their objectives.

It is the same with economic hard power. This can be used to achieve the immediate outcomes a nation state requires, but it can also encourage long-term hostility and resentment. President Trump, for example, is using economic hard power to try to bully Mexico into financing a wall between their two countries, while the Doha Round of WTO trade negotiations has resolved so little because the EU has used its enormous economic influence to block the demands of the developing world for greater access to its agricultural markets. We should beware of taking this argument too far, however. In most instances, economic hard power is enormously useful and need not create an undue backlash. The EU, for example, has also deployed the attractions of its markets to encourage human rights and democracy among African, Caribbean and Pacific countries through the Cotonou Agreement. Equally, the structural adjustment programmes that both the World Bank and the International Monetary Fund impose on countries are generally accepted only because they come with loans, thereby enabling them to further spread the principles of the Washington Consensus globally.

e This paragraph demonstrates clearly that the student knows how to access all three assessment levels. As well as demonstrating knowledge and understanding (AO1), the implications of the material are analytically explored (AO2) and the clever use of the phrase 'We should beware of taking this argument too far' ensures that AO3 is also clearly being delivered.

In spite of this, there are limits to what hard power can achieve. Free-market structural adjustment programmes have caused enormous resentment in developing countries, from Jamaica to Ghana, which has limited the appeal of the Washington Consensus. There are also obvious limits to what military power alone can achieve. In Vietnam during the 1960s and 1970s, superior American military force did not achieve its objectives because it failed in what US Defense Secretary Robert McNamara called the battle to win 'hearts and minds'. In exactly the same way, NATO failed to achieve its objectives in Afghanistan after 2001 since it was unable to construct an effective narrative of events that could win support in Taliban heartlands. In Iraq after 2003 American and British forces, having overthrown Saddam Hussein, were unable to persuade enough of the Iraqi population that they offered a compelling vision of what a future Iraq would look like.

e The use of 'In spite of this' shows that the student understands how important evaluative balance is (AO3). The evidence that is then deployed is well selected and adds to the overall coherence of the writing.

All of this suggests, therefore, that a combination of both hard and soft power (referred to by Joseph Nye as 'smart power') is necessary in order to fully achieve success. Historians point out that the Soviet Union collapsed not only because of its inability to compete with the United States' superior economic and military hard power, but also because President Ronald Reagan, 'the Great Communicator', was able to articulate a much more attractive vision for the future than Communism. The importance of 'whose story wins' has increased with the rise of the internet, since the appeal of what you stand for can be instantly undermined by hostile media coverage, as illustrated by the human rights abuses carried out at the Abu Ghraib US prison in Iraq, which provided Iraqi insurgents with a massive morale boost. More recently, so-called Islamic State has established a significant presence on the internet: interestingly, only a tiny amount of its propaganda is violent — most of it focuses on the sense of community it creates among believers. President Trump's lack of interest in what others think about the United States may, therefore, work to his disadvantage since it may build up yet more dangerous resentment towards the USA, so exacerbating the conflicts American forces are engaged in. Stalin is once said to have quipped, 'How many divisions has the Pope?' Perhaps, today, with the rise of Facebook and Twitter, how many divisions you have matters rather less than it did?

ⓔ In this paragraph the student successfully brings together a number of different threads and weaves them together to create a persuasive interpretation of both the strengths and the limitations of hard power. The last sentence is a little risky, as rhetorical questions don't often work, but here the student just about gets away with it!

In conclusion, it would be naïve to suggest that soft power can be an effective substitute for hard power. There are many occasions when hard power can achieve the necessary results, such as the British intervention within Sierra Leone in 2000 that swiftly ended the civil war there. There are limits on what power alone can achieve, however. Terrorists, for example, can be killed in huge numbers, but unless their appeal is defeated by a superior narrative, there will always be more terrorists to kill. This is something the British government came to realise in the 1990s, which is why it began to negotiate with Sinn Fein in Northern Ireland. Therefore, it seems that stories *do* still matter in international relations and that the most successful nation states, ideologies and institutions of global governance have been those that have been able to inspire confidence while also asserting the sort of hard power that discourages opposition.

ⓔ The conclusion is focused and thoughtful. A clear answer to the question is provided based upon the preceding arguments and counter-arguments.

This essay achieves Level 5 across all the assessment objectives. Its particular strength is that it never stops answering the question and there is a real sense of the evidence being used to build towards a persuasive and deeply considered conclusion. Occasionally the evidence utilised could be a little sharper, but this is a minor criticism of a finely structured, thoughtful and probing essay.

ⓔ **Level 5: 28/30 marks awarded**

Regionalism and the European Union

Question 7

Evaluate the extent to which the European Union is a significant global actor.

You must consider this view and the alternative to this view in a balanced way.   (30 marks)

> **Student answer**
>
> Henry Kissinger's dismissive comment, 'Who do I call if I want to call Europe?'
> provides a powerful reason why realists have often dismissed the European
> Union's potential for global influence. In a world dominated by nation states, the
> EU lacks the unity and nationhood to play more than a marginal role in global
> affairs. Since landmark treaties such as Maastricht (1992) and Lisbon (2007),
> however, the EU has achieved a more unified structure and sense of purpose, to
> the extent that some political commentators see it as representing a powerful
> new focus of power in an increasingly multipolar world.

e This is a snappy introduction, which makes clear that the student appreciates
the main focus of the debate. The Kissinger quotation works well because its
meaning is effectively explored and used as a launching pad into the essay.

> As a result of the Maastricht Treaty, the European Economic Community became
> the European Union with a common citizenship. Maastricht also committed the
> EU to a common currency, as well as to a common foreign and security policy.
> These reforms increasingly provided the EU with the potential characteristics
> of a nation state, making it more likely that it would be able to assert influence
> on the world stage. The Lisbon Treaty further developed the global potential
> of the EU by establishing the positions of a European President and a High
> Commissioner for Foreign Affairs (currently Donald Tusk and Federica
> Mogherini), who would represent the EU in international diplomacy. In addition
> to this the EU was given a legal identity, which means that it now employs its
> own diplomatic staff and has opened up embassies across the world.

e A strength of this paragraph is that it deploys some useful theory about the
relationship between nation states and power, providing powerful AO2 support.
The references to Maastricht and Lisbon are accurate and helpful, further
enhancing both AO1 and AO2.

These reforms have been important in enabling the EU to negotiate with nation states on equal terms. The EU, as a recognisable political entity, is thus represented on the World Trade Organization and also attends meetings of the G7 and the G20. Indeed, the EU's unwillingness to open up its borders to agricultural products from the developing world is one of the key reasons why the Doha Trade Round has been so unsuccessful. More constructively, the EU is playing a pivotal role in combatting climate change. The EU has thus been represented as one body at UN climate change conferences and, by its commitment to reducing carbon emissions by as much as 40 per cent by 2030 compared with 1990 levels, the EU has exercised a remarkable amount of global soft power leadership — consistently more so than either China or the United States.

e This paragraph is strong on AO2 since the student carefully explains ways in which the EU is able to deploy its diplomatic influence within a global context.

We should not exaggerate this point, however. The EU is a very powerful regional body but, unlike a nation state, it does not possess a unified foreign policy. This is because, on the European Council and Council of Ministers, member states still exercise the veto on key areas that define national sovereignty, such as foreign policy and defence. As a result of this, the EU is silent on many global issues because it has not been possible to achieve unity among all its members. Thus, over crises such as the overthrow of Colonel Gaddafi of Libya, the Libyan Civil War, the Russian annexation of Crimea, and the Syrian Civil War and resulting refugee crisis, the EU has been unable to provide leadership because its members have such widely divergent views. For example, EU sanctions against Russia over the annexation of Crimea have not been more hard-hitting because they have had to satisfy all members, including those like Hungary, Italy and Greece that have close economic ties with Russia and so do not wish to antagonise the Kremlin. As Russia's ambassador to the EU, Vladimir Chizhov, put it, 'The EU is not a super-state; it's not a federation; it's still 28 countries.'

e This paragraph clearly demonstrates the student now bidding for AO3 marks since the extent of the EU's global influence is effectively questioned with some probing examples. The quotation is well selected and thought-provoking.

Although these crises have demonstrated that there are considerable limits to what EU diplomacy can achieve, it should be remembered that the EU possesses extraordinary economic power. As the world's largest economy and single trading bloc, worth $20 trillion, the EU's economic hard power is unrivalled, enabling it, for example, to negotiate with the United States on equal terms the Trans-Atlantic Trade and Investment Partnership. The EU has also deployed its massive economic influence to encourage human rights and democracy in the developing world. It does this through the Cotonou Agreement, which requires African, Caribbean and Pacific countries to reach certain standards of political and human rights if they are to gain favourable access to European markets. It has been suggested, too, that EU sanctions on Iranian oil were so hard-hitting that they played a pivotal role in encouraging Iran to agree to limitations on its nuclear programme in 2015 in a treaty to which the EU was a signatory. The immensity of its economic power also provides the EU with particularly strong influence in its near abroad. Turkey has, for example, agreed to take back large numbers of Syrian migrants who have made it to Greece — on the understanding that Turkish nationals will be given access to the Schengen Zone, that talks on Turkish membership of the EU will be 're-energised' and that the EU will give £2.3 billion to Turkey to help it cope with the migrant crisis. Since, too, the EU, as one body, recognises the independence of Kosovo, this has made it impossible for Serbia (or its main backer, Russia) to claim that it is still part of the Serb Federation.

e Strong AO2 continues in this paragraph with the strengths and weaknesses of the case being systematically examined. The detailed analysis of the evidence ensures that AO1 and AO2 are also still much in evidence.

Even though economic hard power can achieve a great deal, realists point out that hard military power still represents the most important metric of global power in an anarchic world system. Here the record of the EU is much less sure. Maastricht, as we have seen, did provide the foundations for a common European foreign and security policy and the President of the European Commission, Jean-Claude Juncker, has argued strongly in favour of a European army. Most members of the EU are also members of NATO, however, and so prioritise their national defence through that organisation. This naturally undermines the military potential of the EU. Since it lacks a nuclear deterrent or a large standing army, the EU is also easily marginalised in global crises where the potential for an overwhelming military response could be of defining significance. Having said that, the EU has now introduced its first rapid reaction force and EU soldiers have been deployed in peace-keeping missions in Kosovo, Bosnia and Macedonia, as well as in the Central African Republic and the Democratic Republic of the Congo. In addition to this, the EU has pooled its naval forces to combat Somali pirates in Operation Atalanta, and has also established a joint naval command to combat people-smugglers operating out of Libya. These, though, are relatively small operations and, given the unwillingness of most EU members to be in what Christopher Coker calls 'the war business', it is unlikely that the EU will ever become a significant global military player, which significantly diminishes its capacity for global influence. Indeed, Zbigniew Brzezinski, President Carter's National Security Adviser, once joked that 'the European Union acts as if its central goal is to become the world's most comfortable retirement home'!

e This paragraph is also very strong in terms of all the assessment levels. The argumentation is really strong and the evidence is thoroughly examined for what it does and does not tell us. The use of the exclamation mark is unusual but, in the circumstances of a strong response, it works really well.

> The EU's capacity to provide global leadership is thus less than one might expect, given its huge size and population. Lacking in unity and militarily weak, it does not have a coherent sense of diplomatic purpose, and in global crises it generally plays second (or even third) fiddle to the Permanent Members of the Security Council. Its influence, though, must not be discounted entirely. Economically a global actor of the first order, its reputation for democracy and human rights also provides the EU with significant soft power influence. The former British Foreign Secretary David Miliband once referred to the EU as a 'model power' that others wish to emulate. It has certainly played this role to perfection over climate change and as the world's largest donor of overseas aid (€75.5 billion in 2016). In an increasingly interdependent world this sort of cultural and economic influence is likely to become ever more important, suggesting that, in spite of its continued political disunity and lack of hard military power, the EU is likely to play an increasingly prominent role in global relations.

e This is a very interesting conclusion, in which the student successfully works the implications of the material through to an entirely persuasive conclusion that is fully justified by the evidence.

The student achieves the top of Level 5 in all assessment levels because of the wide range of precise detail deployed, its ruthless interrogation and the way in which all sides of the argument are thoroughly examined. The essay is pacey, intelligent and thought-provoking, and so achieves full marks.

e Level 5: 30/30 marks awarded

Knowledge check answers

Theories of global politics

1 Realists argue that global politics is anarchic because nation states are accountable to no legitimate higher authority. To survive in such a potentially hostile environment, sovereign states must secure their existence by relying upon being strong in a self-help environment.

2 According to realism, conflict is inherent in global relations because humans are insatiably greedy and this encourages constant strife (classical realism). In addition to this, competition for influence between states in an anarchic world order (neo-realism/ structural realism) creates the conditions for a constant struggle for influence. Attempts by nation states to resolve this problem through military build-up creates a security dilemma, however, in which other states feel threatened, so inadvertently encouraging destabilising arms races.

3 Liberals believe that the realist emphasis on the sovereign self-interest of states is unhelpful. Instead, they view global relations as much more defined by co-operation in pursuit of collective goals by both states and non-state actors. They also dispute the centrality of state egoism and argue that complex interdependence means that a harmonious balance of interests is possible in international relations.

4 Collective dilemmas are worldwide problems, like climate change, that cannot be resolved by states acting alone. Instead they require global co-operation. Liberals argue that the growing number of collective dilemmas is encouraging complex interdependence between states and demonstrating the limitations of the realist approach to international relations.

5 The United Nations Security Council, the International Court of Justice, the International Criminal Court, the UN climate change conferences, the Bretton Woods Institutions (World Bank, IMF, WTO), the G7(8) and G20, and regional organisations like the European Union, all provide examples of global governance. Their effectiveness, though, is undermined by the sovereignty of states since the letter still decide the extent to which it is in their best interests to co-operate with other nation states in organs of global governance.

The state and globalisation

6 Nation states are autonomous and self-governing political entities that are defined by a shared ethnicity, history and culture. According to realism, since there is no authority greater than the nation state, they play the defining role in global politics.

7 Cultural globalisation is controversial because, according to its critics, it encourages blandness, materialism and superficiality as well as, potentially, violent reactions. Its supporters argue that it creates greater empathy between people across borders, so creating the conditions for greater international understanding.

8 Liberals have a favourable approach to globalisation since they view it as a way of enhancing peace and stability by encouraging global co-operation and interdependence. Realists are more sceptical about globalisation since it challenges the authority of the nation state as the key actor in global politics.

9 According to globalisation sceptics, the impact of globalisation has been exaggerated since the nation state remains the primary actor in international relations. Conversely, hyper-globalisers argue that globalisation is dramatically challenging the centrality of the nation state. Transformationalists accept that globalisation is all-encompassing but claim that the nation state can also deploy it to its advantage.

10 Neo-classical economists argue that economic globalisation leads to greater global wealth and prosperity by dramatically increasing international free trade. According to neo-Marxist dependency theory, however, economic globalisation reinforces international structural inequalities by enabling the Global North to exploit the Global South.

Global governance: Political

11 The main functions of the United Nations are to preserve peace, resolve conflict, encourage development, improve human rights and increase respect for international law.

12 The United Nations addresses poverty through a number of Economic and Social Council agencies, such as the World Health Organization and the World Food Programme. Both the Millennium and Sustainable Development Goals have sought to reduce global poverty, as have the associated Bretton Woods Institutions.

13 The United Nations is a liberal organ of global governance. Its principles therefore often conflict with realism, which prioritises the national interest over the collective good.

14 In 1949 NATO was established as a defensive military alliance. Since the end of the Cold War it has become more proactive in protecting Western interests and has intervened in Bosnia (1995), Kosovo (1999), Afghanistan (2003) and Libya (2011).

15 NATO expansion eastwards has been criticised by Russia for being antagonistic. The United States has also been critical of the way in which most NATO countries 'unfairly freeload' off its disproportionate military and economic commitment to the alliance. NATO's external operations have been criticised for being too ambitious and going beyond its basis as a collective security organisation.

Global governance: Economic

16 The International Monetary Fund has three main functions: it provides monetary and financial information and technical support to nation states; it monitors the health and stability of the global economy; in a financial emergency it acts as a lender of last resort.

17 The World Bank encourages development through free-market structural adjustment programmes. Under recent heads of the World Bank, such as Robert Zoellick and Jim Kim, it has also focused on social programmes including gender equality, AIDS prevention, educational reform and small business encouragement. The World Bank is also playing a leading role in debt relief through the Highly Indebted Poor Countries Initiative.

18 The World Trade Organization is controversial because its commitment to free-market economic globalisation has been criticised for reinforcing structural inequalities in global trade. Its lack of a social and environmental agenda (unlike the World Bank) and the way in which the European Union, powerful nation states and influential lobbying groups exert considerable influence on it, have further increased criticism of it, especially in the developing world.

19 According to world systems/dependency theory, neo-classical economic theory (economic globalisation/Washington Consensus) reinforces existing structural inequalities in the global economy. As a result of this, core states in the Global North are able to continue their neo-colonial dominance of peripheral states in the Global South.

20 The orthodox measure of development focuses on economic growth as the key determinant of success. According to alternative models of development, economic well-being is only one facet of development. Development also needs to be measured in terms of social cohesion, gender equality, sustainability, human rights protection and political freedom.

Global governance: Human rights

21 The International Court of Justice (World Court) cannot initiate cases itself and depends upon the co-operation of nation states for its judgments to be enforced.

22 United Nations tribunals (former Yugoslavia, Cambodia, Sierra Leone and Rwanda) have advanced the principle of global accountability for crimes committed within states, laying the foundations for the International Criminal Court. They have also had a retributive function, punishing the crimes of notorious war criminals such as Charles Taylor and Radovan Karadžić, and have developed the principles of human rights-based international law, for example in cases involving rape as a tool of genocide.

23 The effectiveness of the International Criminal Court has been undermined by the number of powerful nation states that do not recognise its authority, so reducing its global legitimacy. Its lack of enforcement power further challenges its authority and its perceived focus on Africa has damaged its reputation in the developing world.

24 According to realism, states act according to sovereign self-interest. This challenges the liberal approach to global politics, which emphasises our common humanity and seeks to establish a universal standard for human rights protection.

25 Liberals justify humanitarian intervention on the moral basis that within the international community there is an 'obligation to save strangers'. More practically, if humanitarian crises are allowed to 'spill over' they can threaten regional and even global stability, while providing a breeding ground for extremism.

Global governance: Environmental

26 Deep ecologists are highly critical of shallow ecology because they believe it is motivated by human selfishness rather than by genuine environmentalism and that it only provides solutions that will enable humankind to keep on exploiting the Earth. Shallow ecologists argue that deep ecology is anti-human and that its aims are so radical and unachievable that they repel support for green issues.

27 Garrett Hardin's concept of the tragedy of the commons shows how the global commons will be exhausted by individual greed if nation states, transnational corporations and consumers continue to prioritise their individual desires over the collective good.

28 UN climate change conferences have been successful in focusing global attention on the problem of climate change and achieving a near-total global consensus that temperature rise in the twenty-first century must be kept as close to 1.5 degrees as possible. The conferences have been much less successful in persuading nation states to accept mandatory cuts to their carbon emissions.

29 The United Nations Framework Convention on Climate Change has increased awareness among nation states that climate change is a 'collective dilemma' that can be resolved only through global co-operation. However, concerted action by the global community continues to be weakened by the realist emphasis on the sovereign self-interest of nation states.

30 Nation states still play the most important role in combatting climate change. Their influence is also being complemented by the decisions made by regional organisations, however, as well as those made by transnational corporations and sub-state actors such as elected mayors, regional governments and consumers themselves.

Knowledge check answers

Power and developments

31 Hard power can be deployed as a form of compulsion through the effective utilisation of military power, the issuing of economic sanctions or promises of future trading rights, and the construction of a balance of power that favours your state over another.

32 A superpower like the United States can make its military, political, economic and cultural influence felt anywhere in the world. Great powers, like Russia, China and the United Kingdom, possess great influence and prestige in global relations but lack the all-encompassing 'mobility' of power that a superpower can claim.

33 According to hegemonic stability theory, a global hegemon discourages conflict because the hegemon provides many of the advantages of a world government by enforcing a global standard of rules that lesser states then bandwagon behind. Critics argue that a 'malign' hegemon can undermine respect for international law since it can act above it if it wishes. Much depends, too, on whether the hegemon's dominance is unchallenged: if it is seen to be weakening, this can lead to the instability of power transition.

34 Realists like bipolarity because they believe it encourages equilibrium, balance and stability by disincentivising conflict. Liberals respond that bipolarity is based upon mutual suspicion, fear and resentment, and so does not provide the foundations for lasting peace.

35 Realists distrust multipolarity because it represents the absence of equilibrium. They believe the constant jockeying for influence by nation states creates the fear and uncertainty that provoke conflict. Liberals, in contrast, believe that multipolarity provides greater opportunities for nation states to co-operate in multilateral organs of global governance, on the model of a college campus.

Regionalism and the European Union

36 Regionalism can be seen to have been encouraged by globalisation. This is because by joining together in regional organisations, nation states can protect themselves more effectively from foreign competition and global security challenges, as well as more effectively representing the views of their members in global negotiations.

37 The North American Free Trade Agreement (NAFTA) is an example of a regional organisation that was established to develop trade and prosperity within a region. The Organization for Security and Co-operation in Europe (OSCE) focuses on maintaining regional stability, while a main focus of the Arab League is to provide the Arab world with a more united voice in global political debate. The European Union (EU) is motivated by all three considerations; so too, to a lesser extent, are the Association of Southeast Asian Nations (ASEAN) and the African Union (AU).

38 By expanding, the European Union risks becoming so economically and culturally heterogeneous that the process of greater integration is diluted. The Lisbon Treaty (2007) tried to resolve the problem of whether the EU can widen and deepen at the same time by establishing new structures to more tightly integrate membership.

39 The European Union possesses a number of supranational bodies, such as the European Commission, the European Parliament, the European Central Bank and the European Court of Justice, which have developed the EU as a single political entity. Nation states still represent their national interests on the Council of Ministers and the European Council, ensuring that the EU maintains an intergovernmental dimension.

40 The European Union can be seen as a unique example of regionalism because it was established as a response to two world wars. It thus possesses a moral imperative that has increased the speed and depth of European integration.

Index